MY FATHER'S AMAZING JOURNEY

of *Faith*

A TRUE STORY / JOURNALS

Sang Sun Lee and
Dr. Stephanie Chung

 FriesenPress

One Printers Way
Altona, MB R0G 0B0
Canada

www.friesenpress.com

ISBN
978-1-03-912970-2 (Hardcover)
978-1-03-912969-6 (Paperback)
978-1-03-912971-9 (eBook)

Biography & Autobiography, Personal Memoirs

Distributed to the trade by The Ingram Book Company

MY DAD'S FAVOURITE SCRIPTURE

"Blessed is the one
Who does not walk in step with the wicked
Or stand in the way that sinners take
Or sit in the company of mockers,

But whose delight is in the law of the LORD
And who meditates on his law day and night.

That person is like a tree planted by streams of water,
Which yields its fruit in season
And whose leaf does not wither—
Whatever they do prospers."

Psalms 1:1–3 NIV

복 있는 사람은
악인들의 꾀를 따르지 아니하며
죄인들의 길에 서지 아니하며
오만한 자들의 자리에 앉지 아니하고

오직 여호와의 율법을 즐거워하여 그의
율법을 주야로 묵상하는도다

그는 시냇가에 심은 나무가
철을 따라 열매를 맺으며
그 잎사귀가 마르지 아니함 같으니 그가
하는모든 일이 다 형통하리로다

시편 1:1-3

1912 – 2020
FOREWORD

My dad was 106 years old when he was interviewed for these journal entries. The entries were printed weekly from August 26, 2017, to March 3, 2018, in *The Christian Times*, a local Korean newspaper distributed across Canada.

My father left his earthly home on September 24, 2020, and is now in the presence of God he loved and served all his days.

My dad's family now consists of four sons (Hyoseob, Yoseob, Yilseob, Paul Kyusup) and two daughters (Sookja and Stephanie Sungja) and their spouses (Yonsoo, Euijung, Heesoon, Peter, Jeongwon, and Ilsim). Three sons are elders, and the youngest serves as a pastor in New York. The two daughters serve in their respective churches and their communities. Two sons-in-law serve as elders. The family also includes eighteen grand-children and fifteen great-grandchildren. Three grandchildren are pastors in New York, Boston, and Seattle. Family members are located in Korea, Canada, and the United States.

I dedicate my dad's story to his growing family
of grandchildren and great-grandchildren.
I pray that his life and story will be a blessing to many.

Stephanie Chung

ACKNOWLEDGEMENTS

Thank you to God for his enduring faithfulness and blessings throughout the generations.

Thank you to my siblings for your unfailing prayers and the support you gave our parents throughout their lives.

Thank you to Pastor Sangho Byun, who generously gave his time to interview my dad and arranged for his story to be published in the newspaper.

Thank you to Susie Chung, my sister-in-law, who translated the entries from Korean to English.

Thank you to *The Christian Times* for publishing my dad's journal entries.

We are grateful to the pastoral staff and congregation of the Vancouver Philadelphia Church for their faithful teaching and prayers.

We are grateful to the staff and residents of Amenida Seniors' Community for the care and love they gave to our parents.

Thank you to Heeyeon Paik, the artist, who painted a portrait of my dad. The photo of the painting is on the cover of this book.

Thank you to Alice Kozier and Louise Dudar for their assistance in editing and submitting the sketches.

PROLOGUE

Just like the man described in Psalm 1:1–3 in the Bible, I tried to live my life without straying from the position of a blessed man.

I lived through the Korean War, and I experienced near-death five different times. Each time I encountered death, I prayed to live. If God would let me live, I promised Him that I would spend the rest of my life building churches.

After fleeing my hometown in North Korea during the war, I ended up in Suwon City in Gyeonggi Province and established roots there.

The first church in South Korea I helped build was Suwon First Church. I was its founding member. The second church I built was also in Suwon. I donated a piece of land and contributed funds to the building of that church. In total, I established at least twenty-five churches around the world during my lifetime.

As a businessman all my life, I should have reinvested the money I made or reserved some money for rainy days. However, every time I saved about five thousand dollars, some minister I did not know from somewhere in the country would appear serendipitously and request a donation to build a church.

Regardless of the denomination, I gave all I had saved from my business to the church, having received the promise that a future church would be planted. Of course, it may have cost more than five thousand dollars to build the entire church, but that money would have purchased ten houses in my area after the war. It was not a small donation at the time.

I would like to return to Korea, but I am too old to travel, and my body does not have the stamina to travel. On the other hand, I don't want to visit Korea because I established a rule for myself when donating monies to the churches. Once I donated the money, there was to be no further contact. That was my rule.

If I were to visit Korea now, I expect former ministers to seek to honour me and repay me. I wish God to receive the honour and glory. For the commemoration of one hundred years of Christianity in Korea, I was asked numerous times by the Korean Business Association to give my testimony about providing financial assistance to build churches. I declined.

I continued my financial support of the churches even when my business was not doing well. Toward the end of my work, there was a minister from Jeju Island who came for help. I had no money at that time and had to send him away empty-handed, except for some out-of-pocket transportation expenses. I still think perhaps I should have taken out a loan to assist him financially. I apologize to that minister as I write this testimony. As I look back, I have some regrets.

My children did not receive an inheritance. The profit from my businesses went to building churches. I had already made prior commitments to support other churches, and I needed to keep the commitments. As a result, I couldn't contribute fully to my children's college education. They all supported themselves with scholarships or part-time jobs.

I am grateful for the assistance of Pastor Sangho Byun, whom I later met in Vancouver. He attended the first church I planted in Suwon and encouraged my early steps at producing this journal.

As an elder, sometimes my memory may fail, please be patient with any inaccuracies. I hope that the readers of my journal will be aware of my sincere heart.

My Journal Entries Printed in
The Christian Times
(The only Christian Korean newspaper printed in Canada)

August 2017-March 2018

JOURNAL ENTRY PUBLISHED AUGUST 26, 2017: MY HOMELAND

Korea, my homeland, is the subject of ongoing news. Before the Korean War, I had no idea what terror was or the magnitude of death and sorrow.

My hometown was in North Korea, in a place called Sariwon in Jangyun Town, located in Eunyul County in Hwanghae Province.

To the west of my town was the Yellow Sea, to the north was Nampo Port on the Daedong River that flowed mightily. To the east was my hometown Sariwon, and to the south was Haeju City.

My hometown was located at the foot of a majestic mountain called Guwol Mountain, which changed its colours annually. It was so beautiful. I had desperately hoped to return to my hometown one day.

I am now well over a hundred years old, and I am losing my short-term memory. Sometimes I can't even remember where I put my phone. However, I still have a vivid memory of my childhood. The mountain, the river, the valleys, the town bridge, and the blooming azaleas are etched in my memory.

If I were to go back, I would take the train to my hometown. It would embrace me, this old, white-haired man, and take me to where my parents are buried. I would then put my head down in front of their burial site and cry with bitterness and joy. I want to tell them what happened to me during the war, how I crossed the 38th parallel while the bullets were flying by me. I would recall the difficulties as a refugee, filled with sorrow. I would tell them everything I endured.

There was a church in Eunyul County, and my father's older brother was one of the two church leaders. My parents also were devoted Christians and attended that church. All our relatives lived in the same neighbourhood, side by side. We lived in harmony. We felt as if we were in heaven.

My last memory of my parents was of them watching me leave my hometown. They were standing on a hill by the poplar tree, waving at me until I was no longer in their sight. Their final words to me were, "You must stay alive, no matter what!"

Now that I am reminiscing about my childhood, I realize my family was rather wealthy compared to everyone else in town. My family owned two large apple orchards, and we were in the business of growing and selling apples, which was extremely lucrative at the time. In the spring, the apple trees blossomed, all in white. In the fall, the white blossoms matured into red apples and the aroma from the apples spread throughout the town.

I miss the sight and smell of those apples, and I love apples to this day. My family had plenty of apples to eat. But most people only had apples during special occasions because apples were rare, expensive, and considered a precious commodity at the time. Because my family had plenty of apples, I became the object of envy of the neighbourhood kids and my school peers. I had two Korean teachers and two Japanese teachers. I became popular with my teachers due to the apples that were delivered to them as presents from my family.

I think about my childhood and hometown a lot, but I cannot recall any bad memories. It was truly an idyllic setting, and I am homesick, wishing to be there one more time. But what can I do, now that I can no longer go back to those days?

JOURNAL ENTRY PUBLISHED SEPTEMBER 2, 2017: MY CHILDHOOD

Thanksgiving will be here in a month or so. I watch the full moon rising and know that this is a season that repeats itself every year. I think of my father and miss him, especially during this season. He was a traditional man, thoughtful and considerate, and extremely affectionate toward his children.

Even though there were more than a hundred children in my neighbourhood, there was no school. Those that could afford to attend school attended the neighbouring village school.

Instead of attending the neighbouring village school, my father decided to provide me with Western education. My elementary school was located in Eunyul County, about five miles away from my home. He decided that it was too far for me to walk back and forth at that age. He divided his land and leased it out to tenant farmers, receiving part of the crop as their rent. My father then rented a tiny room in a farmhouse near my school and got a job as a delivery man, using an ox cart. He had never worked for anybody in his life since he owned his own business, but he took on physical labour so that he could provide me with Western education.

At the end of a long day, he'd often walk into the farmhouse with red bean paste bread for me, purchased with his hard-earned money. When I think of his devotion and dedication toward me, I choke up with tears and can hardly breathe. He worked day and night, doing backbreaking physical labour so that his oldest son could succeed in life. Whenever I eat something delicious that I know my father would like, or travel to new places my father has never been, I picture my father's back pulling the ox cart, and that just makes my heart ache.

We lived like that for about three and a half years until my mother suddenly became ill. We returned to our hometown. By then, I was in the fourth grade. My father then bought me a bicycle to commute to and from school. Bicycles were expensive at that time, and only a few rich Japanese children were riding them. I rode my bike with much pride, ringing the bicycle bell loudly around my neighbourhood as I commuted, with other children watching me with envy.

I was also given many musical instruments, procured by my father from the missionaries. In an effort to pass down his unwavering faith to me, my father wanted me to learn to play the instruments. Whenever he received news about some instruments brought in by the missionaries, he'd purchase them, even if he had to sell a cow for the price. Some instruments he bought were a piano, a flute, and a trumpet. He learned how to play them and then gave me lessons.

Soon after learning to play the instruments, I led a music performance at a big gathering of many churches. I was eighteen years old and a bachelor when I became a church choir director and a deacon. My father's faith was already bearing the fruit of his spiritual labour.

JOURNAL ENTRY PUBLISHED SEPTEMBER 9, 2017: ADULTHOOD AND STARTING THE BUSINESS

As a teenager, I played in the stream pouring down from the Kuwol Mountain, fishing and swimming in it. Before I knew it, I was a twenty-year-old adult.

Being a twenty-year-old now is very different from being a twenty-year-old then. The twenty-year-olds then had more responsibilities, and therefore had to be more mature. I became the head of my family at that age, taking care of all matters concerning the family. My father was too old, and as his first son, he handed down all his duties to me.

I went to Pyongyang frequently to sell apples grown in our orchard. Pyongyang was where all the businessmen and peddlers gathered from all over the country at the time. I did not have the business acumen they did and did not have the business skills they did. I was a small-time country boy. But, because I had received a Western education, I gained high respect from the big bosses. They gave me due respect and credit, and as a result, I was never caught in the middle of any fraudulent deals.

It took two to three hours by train to get from Nampo Port to Pyongyang. But I had too many apples to take on the train. The shipment cost by train would have been exorbitant. So, I rented a boat and filled it with apples, using the TaeDong River as my highway, and transported the apples for sale. The boat trip took about three days. We sailed the boat using the wind, and the sailors were remarkable in their navigation skills. Even though I rented the boat at first, I later bought my own boat with a friend. The apple business was lucrative.

Pyongyang was bigger than Nampo Port at that time. There was a saying at the time that if you are in Pyongyang, even the dogs in the street carry money in their mouths. That describes the vibrant scene of the city, which was crowded with businessmen and well-dressed, good-looking Japanese men, crowding around the streets of the city. You could buy anything you needed and anything you wanted. The city offered a variety of food and entertainment, and it overflowed with vitality.

Whenever my father had big business deals, he always sent me on his behalf, saying that his first son naturally would represent him for a successful deal. He relied on me and trusted that I would not be defrauded.

However, those were scary and oppressive times, with Japan occupying Korea as its colony. Every day, my family and I feared receiving the draft notice to serve in the Japanese government. I was only twenty years old, and we saw women being drafted as comfort women, and men being drafted into the Japanese military. Every day, the enlistment notices arrived in our hometown from some big city, and the daily transfer of Korean men and women out of our hometown made my parents pray and cry out to God.

They prayed that I would not be drafted, that I would get married, which would delay the draft. Being married would allow me to carry on the family name and lineage as the oldest son in the family. One prayer led to another, and my parents found a young lady in a small town called Ildo, two small hills away from my hometown. Her family shared the same faith as mine, and the young woman was from a good family background. The marriage was arranged between the parents.

JOURNAL ENTRY PUBLISHED SEPTEMBER 16, 2017: MARRIAGE AND LEARNING THE BUSINESS

Those were the days when you met and saw your bride for the first time at the wedding. But the in-laws asked me to come a few days earlier to be measured for the wedding outfit I was to wear, and that was the first time I met my bride-to-be. She was quiet but warm and gave me a shy smile. My heart was pounding as I saw her, but I thought to myself that I was good husband material. I had the confidence that I could take care of her, by sailing across the TaeDong River, selling premium apples. I thought I would bring her bags of money, and she could avoid any hardship for the rest of her life. I was confident that she would forever enjoy an opulent lifestyle as my wife.

If it weren't for the tragic Korean War that started on June 25, 1950, I probably was right in my thinking; but the war broke out and crushed everything.

Time went by fast, and I was already thirty years old and had become a husband and father of three children. My father, not a strong man anymore, was ageing and fading in energy. And even though we were living through the Japanese colonial era, I was now the head of the family and the family business.

I combined my educational background with the skills I learned from my father. I went full speed ahead with the apple business. Not only was I managing and running the big apple orchard my father owned, but I also bought another orchard and purchased a couple of pieces of land in the mountains for future use.

Many people in my hometown praised my work ethic and combined with sincerity and integrity. My assets had increased. The premium apples that my apple trees produced were popular and desired. The premium apples had to be bright red and plump. So, as the apples ripened, we trimmed the branches and leaves around the apples to bring more sunshine directly to the apples. Eight out of ten apples we grew received the premium grade mark. One box of premium apples was the same price as one big straw bag of rice. These apples were like gold in their value, and we were exporting our apples to Japan. One big apple tree could produce one hundred boxes of apples, and it was God's blessing in every way.

I was able to get into the wholesale business, where the apples were distributed throughout the country. By today's standards, the amount of business I handled was at the same level as that of conglomerates. Whenever I arrived in Pyongyang with my ship brimming with apples, people always offered me cigarettes and alcohol. But I flatly declined them, as I learned from my father not to smoke or drink as a Christian. I would tell them that I was a Christian, and this caused them to trust me all the more while doing business with me.

I usually went to Pyongyang two to three times a month, but I never slept over in Pyongyang. I always took the train to Nampo Port to spend the nights. This was because I didn't want to get too close to people that were out of town. If I had stayed overnight in Pyongyang, we would inevitably end up going in and out of a famous geisha house.

I was abiding by the lessons I learned from my parents to never get into a situation that might shake my faith. That was their way of managing and keeping their faith intact.

I have learned many life lessons from my father. The most important lesson I remember is to keep faith in God, and to look after God's servants and the churches. I have tried to practice the lessons I learned to this day.

The gospel started spreading in Pyongyang, and as time went by, the gospel spread to our villages and hometown. More and more people started attending churches. There were not many churches during that period, so there was no competition among the churches to bring in members as we have now.

Every pastor in every church refused to participate in Shinto worship. So they were taken to prisons and tortured, which caused the church members to pray for the pastors all the more. This was an ongoing occurrence, and my father took special care of those tortured pastors and devoted himself to them. No pastor that ever visited our home left empty-handed. That was another lesson from my father that paved ways for my receiving many blessings.

JOURNAL ENTRY PUBLISHED SEPTEMBER 23, 2017: AVOIDING THE DRAFT AND WORKING FOR THE JAPANESE GOVERNMENT

My parents and my wife worried about me getting drafted into the Japanese military. Many of our hometown friends and neighbours were drafted. The young women were drafted as comfort women, and the young men were drafted to serve in the Japanese military. Those that were poor and had no power or money were the first ones taken by force. Watching them forced to go broke our hearts. Then came my turn. I received the draft that had been postponed all these years. My family and I had used all means available to avoid the draft, but it was no longer going to be delayed. The whole family had spent many hours praying and crying over this issue for years, and when we received the draft notice, we prayed again.

The only way to get out of this draft situation was to become a public official and work for the government. But the status of being a government servant under Japanese rule was not viewed favourably by other Koreans, and I would have to live with the reputation of being pro-Japanese as if I had betrayed my own country.

Given no choice to avoid the draft, I chose the most favourable area of the government service, which was to join the office of forestry. I took the civil servant examination, passed it, and got assigned to Gangwon Province, north of the 38th parallel in North Korea.

I had avoided being drafted into the military, but I had to leave the family apple business, my parents, my wife, and my children and spend a year in the middle of nowhere deep in the mountains. I spent more hours praying than working. This was God's way of providing me with the time and space to build up my faith through prayer.

While I was in the mountains, alone and away from my family, enduring the pain of separation and not knowing when this would all end, my family pursued another position. They wanted me closer to the family, as did I. They found out the examination date for an office clerk position in my hometown, which I took and passed.

I finally came home and was assigned to work in our hometown district office, still avoiding the draft into the military. The fact that I worked as a government official for the Japanese government for three years, from the end of the colonial period to the day Korea was liberated from Japan in 1945, has become part of my résumé.

I received tremendous support from my hometown people. They did not look down on me for taking the government position. They knew I loved my hometown and my family and understood where my heart lay. Even now, I still appreciate the understanding and support I received during that period. I was earnest and dutiful in my position.

During my post as a government official, I felt like Zaccheus, a chief tax-gatherer in the Bible. He was confident that he hadn't cheated anyone and swore to Jesus that he would give back four times as much if he had defrauded anyone of anything. I was as confident as Zaccheus that I hadn't done anything wrong serving in my post as a government official.

At the end of the Japanese colonial period, the government's demand to receive a certain production quota from Koreans was unusually high. Most people in my hometown couldn't meet the demands of the quota. So, I evenly distributed what my family had to the town folks, and as a result, we met the quota and overcame the hardship together.

Of course, all of us spent many hours in tears, sometimes staying up all night praying for Korea's future, asking God to liberate Korea from Japanese rule. A few months before the actual liberation in 1945, some Japanese whom we were close to whispered in our ears that Japan was going to be destroyed soon.

JOURNAL ENTRY PUBLISHED SEPTEMBER 30, 2017: KOREA'S LIBERATION FROM JAPAN

As my family was enduring the hardships of avoiding the draft, Korea was liberated from Japan on August 15, 1945. The sound of people cheering reverberated throughout Eunyul County in Hwanghae Province. It still echoes in my ears. It is an unforgettable emotion.

Everybody ran out into the streets with Korean flags, and the Japanese we had feared like sharp knife blades all disappeared from our sight. Koreans held hands, finding warmth and comfort from each other for having endured severe hardship under Japanese rule. I thought I would now go back to having a life of my own, taking care of the family affairs as the head of the household. I was looking forward to happier times ahead.

One day, five years later, there was a strange feeling in the air. I asked my father to go and deliver a shipment of apples to a distributor in Pyongyang. But he returned home without the shipment, and said he left the shipment with someone else. He said the war had broken out on June 25, 1950. Everybody in Pyongyang had left, seeking refuge somewhere else, and there were lines of people in the street trying to flee the city. As he was talking about what was going on, I heard the loud noises of air bombs, along with the sounds of cannons going off in the distance. The war broke out right before my very eyes.

JOURNAL ENTRY PUBLISHED OCTOBER 7, 2017:
THE KOREAN WAR

The Korean War overshadowed my entire hometown. Everybody was gripped with fear. As the head of the family, I took my bicycle and rode fast toward Nampo Port to find out what was going on. There were hundreds of people in the street, but the Korean National Army uniformed officers told those fleeing that the war was over since they had won, and that the people should all return to their homes. Something was not right.

The war just broke out. It could not have just ended overnight. I rode my bicycle faster toward Nampo. Some soldiers in National uniforms, speaking with a North Korean accent, stopped me with their guns and demanded that I give up my bicycle. These were the North Korean People's Army dressed in the National Army uniform. I refused to surrender my expensive bike and rode past the flying bullets. That was my first encounter with death. Of course, they beat me and took my bicycle by force. I walked home, limping all the way.

I was worried about my family, and all I could see was the image of my family waiting for me as I was dragging myself home. I didn't even know that I had a broken leg. This was war.

Soon after that incident, one of the first lieutenants for the National Army from my hometown left his unit and came home, worried sick about his family. He organized about thirty young men from our town, and we decided to create a civilian army of our own to protect our hometown and families. We were not in the army, but civilians, and we were now fighting the North Koreans in North Korea. We were renegades. None of us were in a position to choose which army to join. If we decided to join the North Korean People's Army, we'd have to fight the National Army coming from the south. If we chose to join the National Army, we'd have to fight the North Korean army. Either way, we were doomed.

If we were going to be doomed and die anyway, we decided we'd die fighting to protect our families. Our only weapon was one gun that the first lieutenant had in his possession. That was it.

The civilian army we formed found an operation centre on a remote island at the far end of the East Sea. We strategized in detail. We even made reckless decisions to gather weapons from the enemies with our own bare hands. We were clever in grabbing the weapons from the enemies coming into the island, looking for us. We accumulated a lot of guns and weapons.

Every day, the fighting was fierce. There was no guarantee we would be alive by the end of the day. I had to witness many of my civilian comrades die right in front of me, fighting the brutal war.

Every time the bullets flew by me, I thought I was going to die then and there. I offered a prayer, "Please let me escape to the South, and if you let me live, I will build churches!" I offered this prayer every time I thought I was going to die.

I knew the geography of my hometown and the surrounding area, which was a big advantage in navigating during the war. That was how I became part of the civilian army, with no military name tags or numbers.

One time, five of us left the island and went into town to get some food and supplies. We were captured by the enemy force. They lined us up, side by side, and started shooting one by one. I was the fourth one in line.

When my turn came to be shot, somebody behind the shooter said in a North Korean accent, "Turn his pockets inside out and see what's in there." There wasn't anything important in my pockets, but the next thing I heard was, "Let him live!" For a few seconds, while this was happening, I poured out my heart to God in prayer to let me live. God heard me and let me live.

A few days after that incident, more than ten of us left the island to get some supplies. This time, we were in the forest, and we were completely surrounded by the enemy force. We lay low, hardly breathing, hiding from the enemy. We heard footsteps nearby and then heard loud voices saying, "If you come out with your hands up, we will let you live." I held my friend's hand next to me and gave him a look that said, "Don't you go out there." He listened to me and did not go out.

The few that believed the enemy got up and went out from hiding with their hands raised. They were massacred with bullets. Those of us who stayed hiding had to witness the brutality right in front of us. The eyes of those that were shooting did not look like those of humans.

What was I struggling to pray at that moment? One little cough would have sent hundreds of bullets toward those of us hiding. I vowed to keep the promise I had already made to God.

The combat continued every day, back to back. The elite troops of the North Korean People's Army were selected, and they all went toward the south. The remaining troops attacked us non-stop. We resisted and did not surrender or give up the fight. We actually did not have time to make a choice, as the attacks continued without a break.

Every day was a battleground. Every day somebody close to me died fighting. We would retreat at times and attack at other times. We had the island as our base operation centre, but when the battles were long, and the food and supplies ran out, we had to go inland.

One time we went inland, we were surrounded by the enemy. We thought we were all going to die but found an underground tunnel. We stayed there in hiding for two nights. When all was quiet, we left the tunnel and ran toward the island. As we were running, we saw three dead bodies on the road. They were covered with blood. Those three that died had gone ahead of us and had stepped on a land mine planted by the enemy. If we had gone ahead of them, we would have been the ones dead. Instead, we lived because of them, and when I realized this, I wailed and wept bitterly.

After a year of experiencing the war at the front and centre of our daily lives, the United Nations found out about us. The United States warship came to the island to take us to the south.

JOURNAL ENTRY PUBLISHED OCTOBER 14, 2017: LEAVING NORTH KOREA

I left a written note on a piece of paper saying I was leaving the island for the south. I had no choice but to leave behind my hometown, my parents, my wife, a two-year-old son who just started to walk, a four-year-old daughter, and a six-year-old son. The tears that ran down my cheeks as I was getting on the warship were mixed with joy, sadness, and prayers. As the ship was leaving the island, and with the land I loved was getting farther and farther away from my view, I wailed and did not hold back my tears. The tears I shed that day felt like tears of blood running down my cheeks. I vowed and prayed that I would build churches when I reached the south.

Two nights later, we arrived at Mokpo Port. I had five cents in North Korean currency in my pocket, which was useless in the south. I had no money for food, and there was no place for me to stay. There was no shelter for me to avoid the misty rain that came down like wet dew. In that situation, I wondered how I could have promised to build churches in return for my life. It was like a scene from the Bible where Jacob was going to live with his uncle with nothing in his pockets.

Sang Sun Lee and Dr. Stephanie Chung

JOURNAL ENTRY PUBLISHED OCTOBER 21, 2017: LIFE AS A REFUGEE IN SOUTH KOREA

I got myself a job lifting and moving straw rice sacks all day. Many refugees had worked similar jobs. After a full day's work, I received two cups of rice as my pay. I was not accustomed to doing hard labour. My body ached to the point where I thought it would fall apart and that I'd die soon. Every day I was consumed with worries about my family I had left behind.

I heard through the grapevine that a distant relative of mine was operating a small business as a street vendor in Yeongdong Market in Suwon City, in Gyeonggi Province. As soon as I heard that news, I went to Suwon. Suwon City became my second hometown.

A street vendor puts down straw mats in front of somebody else's store and pays some money to the owner inside for the space outside. The owner sells items inside that are more profitable, like bars of soap, towels, clothes, and shoes. The street vendor in front of the store sells items like thread, buttons, rubber bands, needles, and small items for everyday use. I was not the owner but an outside vendor. My job was to pick up trash and clean the surrounding area. If it rained, I had to cover the items outside with vinyl to not become wet. I'd get soaked in the rain, but the items remained dry. I did this job as if my life depended on it. Frequently, I was scolded loudly by the owner, and the payment for my work at the end of the day was a bowl of noodles.

The refugees from the north all lived in such poverty. Each day we were rattled by the cannons shooting in the ongoing war. I heard of people dying. There was constant talk of who had died and how they had died. There were so many deaths. I became accustomed to hearing about death to the point of numbness. But when I heard the orphaned children cry, I almost went mad thinking of my own children I had left behind. Those who had to leave our hometown were very eager to receive news about our hometown, even in our displaced state. If anyone spoke with a North Korean accent, we'd run over and ask what town that person was from. It was mostly a useless exercise, but that was the reality of our daily lives during the war. Nobody smiled. Everybody cried. We cried so often, and our eyes were always puffy.

One year passed living in that condition. Then Seoul was reclaimed by South Korea, and my distant relative, the owner of the street vendor, left for Seoul. Before leaving for Seoul, the owner transferred the ownership to me, and I became the street vendor with a few inventory items. I was now the owner of the shop, but my daily life remained about the same.

Two widows ran a boarding house nearby. It was the cheapest in Suwon, occupied mainly by the refugees. Each room was about six and a half by six and a half feet, and three people shared one room. In the winter, we were snug with the warmth of our body heat, but it was so hot in the summer. We had fleas and lice that crawled on our bodies, and there was no way of avoiding them. We had no bathhouses and no facilities to do our laundry.

Some women became experts in catching the lice that were buried in clothes and even exchanged that labour for something in return. In the spring, the men would take off their clothes, sit under the sun, and watch the women catch the lice. There is a saying that there usually are three sacks of rice in a widow's house but only three bags of lice in a widower's house. Our situation reflected that saying.

Even though everyone everywhere experienced sadness, despair, and poverty, there was a difference between the Christians and the non-believers. The believers had the privilege and the blessing of having God to pray to and to trust in the midst of the crisis. I was a believer, trusted God to pull me through this crisis, and did not cease praying. My faith in God was steadfast.

JOURNAL ENTRY PUBLISHED OCTOBER 28, 2017: STARTING SUWON FIRST CHURCH

About ten refugees started a church, and I became one of the founding members. We formed the first church in Suwon—Suwon First Church.

I saved pennies here and there running the street vendor shop, and I was able to contribute to the church building fund with the first small pile of money I had saved working in South Korea. I now had a small community of Christians that I felt close to and with whom I could pray. I experienced the grace of God.

At times, I missed my family so much. I got all worked up worrying about how they were doing, whether they were alive, and if they were okay. I wasn't eating food with pleasure. I forced myself to swallow the food in front of me with tears in my eyes. When this happened, I prayed to God sincerely, asking my family to live so that I could see them again someday. I prayed that I would overcome the negative effects of this war and live.

I practiced what I had learned from my father, which was to form and maintain good relationships with the people in life. I also practiced being a Christian, showing kindness and sincerity in my everyday life. Before I knew it, I became well-known in Yeongdong Market as a man from Hwanghae Province. I spent almost a year living in the same location in Gyeonggi Province, and I became familiar with the area. I went from knowing no one when I first arrived to knowing a small community of church members, the market merchants, and they became my friends.

Even as we were getting used to our new daily life, helping each other and trying to keep our optimism, those of us who had fled from the north experienced extreme loneliness. Often, we'd catch each other gazing at the sky toward the north. We were constantly reminded of the family and friends left behind.

JOURNAL ENTRY PUBLISHED NOVEMBER 4, 2017:
MY WIFE AND THREE CHILDREN FROM THE NORTH

One day, I caught sight of a homeless-looking woman wandering near my store. She was carrying her belongings on her head, had a baby on her back, and her two hands held one child each. She was walking toward me. That was a familiar daily sight during that time, so I didn't pay much attention at first. But as she approached me, my heart stopped. This was my wife and the three children I had left behind in North Korea!

The whole thing didn't make any sense at first. I didn't know if I was dreaming or if this was actually happening. I took my children and my wife into my arms, and we looked at each other, unable to speak for a long time. People started gathering around us, realizing what was happening, and started yelling that a miracle had occurred. Before we knew it, a huge crowd had gathered, and we all started crying with tears that ran down our cheeks like heavy rain. We kept repeating, "Thank you, God. Thank you!"

For those of us who live by faith, there are many things that happen in our lives that cannot be explained. How can a young woman cross the 38th parallel with the South and North Korean armies pointing guns at each other? Crossing alone would be impossible, let alone crossing it with three little children.

After we gained our bearings, we rented a little room. Watching my three children lie down side by side in the room, I felt like a rich man. I asked my wife how she crossed the 38th parallel and found me.

My father in Hwanghae Province sold his entire apple orchard, which he loved so much as if his life depended on having it. But he sold it for all cash and one day sat my wife down with the pile of money and said, "Use this money to go to the south and find your husband. That is the only way for you and your children to survive. There is a rumour that he is staying at Mokpo Port. Start there, and look for him." And then he made a money belt out of the cash, wrapped it around her waist, and made her look like a pregnant woman.

My father then said, "From this point on, your mother-in-law and I will be fasting and praying unceasingly until you arrive safely in South Korea." He then prayed for her to make a safe journey. He was crying so hard; he could hardly speak in his prayers. He blessed her and practically pushed her out the door to leave for the south.

From our hometown, she went to Haeju city and found an underground guide known in the black market as the best of the best among guides. My wife showed him all the money she had in her possession and promised to pay him with everything she had if he could help her and the children cross the 38th parallel safely. The guide had never seen so much money in his life. He wanted to make that money, even if his life was at risk. He made a promise that he would take the job. In the darkness, with my wife's determination that she would find her husband and the children would find their father, they charged in a rush toward the 38th parallel.

During the day, they hid in the mountains. During the night, in the pitch darkness, they walked, falling down at times and hearing hundreds of bullets flying toward those trying to cross the 38th parallel. If they heard any footsteps of the North Korean People's Army nearby, my wife would put her hand on the youngest son's mouth, the guide would put his hand on the second daughter's mouth, and the oldest son would put his own hand on his mouth, all to be quiet and not get caught. They spent three nights crawling through the thorn bushes and in between the rocks. They ignored their hands and feet that bled from crawling and walking. My wife said she prayed, "Lord, I can die, but please let the children live!" At times she'd shout out her prayers, and she'd forget that she was cold and hungry and marched on.

It was God's grace, and not human strength, and her maternal instinct to protect the children that brought her to the south.

As soon as they crossed the 38th parallel to the south, she gave the guide all the money that was wrapped around her waist. She then requested him to deliver the message to her father-in-law that they had arrived safely, thanks to his prayers.

From that point, my wife and children went to Mokpo Port. They spent ten days looking for me. A dock worker at the port said somebody with my name had gone to Suwon Yeoungdong Market. Hungry and tired, looking like beggars, my wife and children changed direction and walked all the way to the market to find me.

My wife slept for two days and ate nothing. She was exhausted. I felt a wave of guilt for her hardship as I watched her sleep as if I had caused all this trouble. Then for months, I couldn't sleep at night, thinking about my father, who had sold everything he had cultivated and accumulated during his lifetime so that I could reunite with my wife and children. My father was that kind of person.

Everybody at that time was living in poverty. Living alone as a refugee seems easier, but having my family with me gave me the strength to carry on. To feed the children until they were full was always our biggest daily task. We sent them to bed early on some nights without food, and we told them not to run around during the day so that they wouldn't become hungry too soon. I was busy trying to make ends meet and ran around here and there to make a little more money to feed the three children. And before I knew it, ten months had passed, living together as a family in the south.

We expanded our store with more items to sell, and life was becoming a bit easier. We enrolled the children in Suwon Jydong Elementary School. We also belonged to a church that was part of our daily lives. And in the evenings, we could sit around in our room and whisper and murmur together as a family.

One day, my wife said she couldn't digest food and that her stomach hurt. We didn't have any hospitals around us, and even if there were any, we had no money to pay for the visit. We went to a nearby Oriental Medical Clinic. The doctor treated her with acupuncture needles and gave her some herbal remedies to take at home. She was sick for two days, and then she collapsed. She then gathered all her strength, and through her difficult breathing, she said, "I brought you our three children from the north. I did my duty, and God fulfilled my mission." She held my hand that night and died and went to heaven, never to return to me.

I wanted to die right then and there with her. She had risked her life crossing the 38th parallel for me. I felt it was my fault that she went through such hardship. My heart overflowed with such sorrow, and I couldn't stand it.

For the first time in my life, I asked God, "What is happening?" No, that question didn't matter. I just broke down and cried until I could cry no more. My three children cried with me. The church members came over, and they cried. The entire Yeongdong Market cried. If my father had witnessed this event, he would have cried more than all of us put together.

We held a sad funeral with hearts ready to burst with grief. It was as if my wife's passing added insult to injury for all of us. Experiencing the war and our life as refugees and being poverty-stricken was almost more than we could bear. Everything felt unreal, and we lived in despair. How could something like this happen?

Silently, with no parting words and with constant tears, we buried my wife. When I came home, my four-year-old son insisted that he go and see his mother. At his young age, he didn't understand that he would never see his mother again. I couldn't drink or eat for several days. I had no desire to do anything and thought about everything that I didn't do for her and couldn't do for her.

At that time, Suwon First Church was a pioneer church, and even though the membership was small in number, everybody chipped in as if my problems were their own. Some brought two sacks of barley, some brought several rolls of noodles, and some even brought a sack of brand-name flour. I can still vividly see all the rare food items people brought to the funeral.

I had been so happy, having reunited with my wife and children. But now, I was a poor displaced refugee widower from the north with three young children.

I carried my youngest son on my back while working at the street vendor shop and sent the two older children to school during the day. Every time I prayed those days, tears would flow down so much that my eyes were always puffy.

JOURNAL ENTRY PUBLISHED NOVEMBER 11, 2017:
MY LIFE AS A WIDOWER

It was not easy for me to raise the three children alone, and at the same time carry on the business, trying to make a living. At that time, sending the children to elementary school required tuition payments.

I had to gather the daily food for the children and buy the necessary firewood to cook the food, so I had no time to wash them and clothe them properly. When the weather became cold, I couldn't do any laundry, and there was no extra clothing to change into. They had to wear the same jacket for three to four months at a time. It was a pitiful sight.

All the roads were muddy. When it rained, the roof leaked. In the evening, the rats came out and ran around in the ceiling, making noises. The floor of our room was uneven, covered with patches of laminated papers.

Many children in the neighbourhood were severely malnourished. Many had bloated bellies as a result of malnourishment. We all lived in poverty and in unsanitary conditions. Everybody was so hungry all the time.

Although the war had just ended, the government was in disarray and could not provide any assistance to the public. Many children became ill. The most common ailment the children suffered was the stomachache. This was because they had roundworms living in their stomachs.

Sometimes during the night, the worms would escape from the children's mouths as they were sleeping. Sometimes several worms, three to four inches long, would come out with their feces, which of course, caused the children to faint from fright.

Many children died when we were faced with contagious diseases. There were no government or any other agencies that could look after these children. We lost many precious young lives that would have been our future foundation for the country.

With desperate living conditions, the children had runny noses all the time. Usually, on the first day of school, the mothers would pin the handkerchiefs to their children's uniforms. My children did not have the luxury of a mother pinning the handkerchiefs on their uniforms. They used their sleeves to wipe their noses, so much so that both of their sleeves were shiny.

The runny nose became a running joke among the young children. They even came up with a riddle: "What are the two old men doing as they go in and out of a cave all day?" There were no tissues to wipe the long runny nose so that the kids would suck up the mucous back into their noses, and this went on all day as they went about their business. My children were especially good at dealing with their runny noses.

Many children became orphans during the war. They roamed the streets, begging and providing for themselves. My children had no mother. When the older two left home for school in the mornings, I could see their jacket sleeves shining with dried mucous, their pants patched with my own awkward sewing by hand. There were patches on the back of their pants and patches on their knees, all of which I sewed to cover up the holes. We used to classify the beggars in three levels: high level, mid-level, and low level. My children resembled low-level beggars. They were the worst of the lot.

Although I had come from the north with nothing, not knowing a soul in the south, I was very grateful to God that I had a little store that sold a few items each day to feed my children. At the time, my total assets consisted of my three children and my faith in God.

One of the hymns we used to sing was about being content, living wherever we were placed, whether in a straw hut or in a big mansion. My home was the straw hut, and I was grateful.

JOURNAL ENTRY PUBLISHED NOVEMBER 18, 2017: ARRIVAL OF A NEW YOUNG WIFE FROM THE SOUTH

One day, a beautifully dressed young woman came to my home. Her body had a scent of body cream that was popular at the time. She was twenty-two years old and pretty. I thought she was the children's teacher from their school coming to do a welfare check and provide guidance. My children often appeared in school unwashed and dressed like beggars. I greeted the young woman and said, "Oh, the lady came!" Before I could stop her, she walked right into my living area infested with rats, lice, and fleas. I could tell by her appearance that she had been raised in a well-to-do house. I could see that her hands did not have any roughness to them, which meant she was not used to working hard.

As she pushed herself inside my living quarters, she looked at the three children with their unwashed faces and said, "Starting today, I will be married into this house and become your mother!" Her announcement was like a bombshell. I was having a hard time trying to make ends meet each day, and now this woman was making my life harder.

She came from an upper-class family in the city of Pyeongtaek. She was the first of six children, and in her social position, she could have married anyone she wanted. But at age eighteen, she became filled with the Holy Spirit and experienced the fireball power of the Gospel. She lived with the joy of knowing God and refused to marry anyone who was not a Christian. She vowed to live alone if no Christian husband appeared. She proclaimed her wish to her parents, and despite the social and family pressure to marry at that age, she went to Suwon City to temporarily stay with a relative.

While staying with her relative, she heard a story from a woman peddler who went door to door selling women's fancy items. The story was about me.

The peddler told her, "There is a widower who came from the north. He was a refugee and went through a very difficult time. He runs a little store in Yeongdong Market in Suwon. His wife escaped to the south from the north with their three children, but then his wife died shortly after that. He is a poor widower, raising three children all by himself. It's such a pitiful sight."

As soon as the young woman heard the story, she heard God's voice saying, "Get married into that household and become a mother to those three children!"

The young woman immediately ran over to the market, verified who I was, and then prayed. She prayed until she received absolute confirmation from God. This is how she ended up coming into my life. She said her decision was final and that I should permit her to marry me, the poor widower.

This was an outrageous request, and at first, I flatly declined. I had kept my faith in God and had looked after myself with God's help. I wasn't going to be convinced or even shaken by this young woman.

I told her to leave, but she didn't leave. I yelled at her for being immature. She didn't blink. I then tried to be nice and explained that what she said didn't make any sense. Nothing I said dissuaded her from her decision.

I came up with an idea and said, "If your parents give you permission, I will think about it," knowing there was no way her parents would allow her to marry me. She then went back home to Pyeongtaek and told her parents everything. They threw a thunderous fit, but it was to no avail. She was unshaken, steadfast in her decision.

Then one day, I was told the woman's father was going to come and meet me. I said to myself, "Good thing! If I meet her father, I will tell him to take the young woman home and explain that she is not acquainted with the way of the world. She's still very innocent, and she doesn't know what she is talking about." I was going to straighten out this misunderstanding. The woman's father came alone. As expected, he started talking in opposition to his daughter's idea of marrying me. He said, "First, you are seventeen years older than she is. Second, you have no money. Third, you are a widower with three young children. Fourth, people in the south consider people from the north as low class. Fifth, the thing I hate most is people who are Christians."

I said, "I agree with everything you said. Please take your daughter home with you!"

He then got teary and said, "My most respected older brother in the family, who passed away a few years ago, came into my dream last night and said, 'Have your daughter marry that widower in Yeongdong Market!'" The woman's father said he always listened to his brother and never went against his wishes.

He then rose from his seat and said, "From today on, I have thrown my daughter out of my house, so do whatever comes next!" As he was walking away from me, I stood watching his back and watched him wipe away his tears with a handkerchief. From the back, he looked just like my own father in Hwanghae Province. The memory of watching him go that day is still vivid in my mind.

I first prayed, as is my custom. I then sought advice from the church elders and fellow believers to determine God's will in my life. I was encouraged to accept the events happening before me as God's providence and received advice to start life afresh with the young woman. We didn't have money for a wedding. We had a simple meal at our church with the other church members and started our new life together. Of course, from that point on, my wife could not visit her family for the next thirteen years.

We were very poor and had difficulty making ends meet. But what was so definitely different was the way the three children were cared for. I don't know where she got the materials to make clothes for the children. She made all the clothes by hand, and the children wore new clean clothes every month, no longer looking like dirty beggars. People around us in the market sometimes didn't recognize the children. My new wife cared for the children and kept them clean.

Even the homeroom teacher called us to school to ask about the changes in the children. Previously, they were the dirtiest kids in school, and it surprised the teacher when they came to school dressed like royalty. I explained to the teacher that their stepmother was doing all the work for the children. The praises of my wife spread throughout the streets of Yeongdong Market and throughout the city of Suwon.

That woman is sleeping next to me right now as I write my testimony. She has lost most of her memory, as she currently suffers from Alzheimer's disease. She reminds me of Lydia in the Bible, the dealer of purple cloths, who helped establish a church in Philippi. This woman spent her entire life in the service of God and produced three children with me. People say I did God's work, but she did all the work with her dedication and sacrifice from where I stand.

JOURNAL ENTRY PUBLISHED NOVEMBER 25, 2017:
THE BIG FIRE

When I was finally beginning to heal from all the pain I had experienced and started a new life with my wife, another unexpected event occurred. We had a big fire in the market one day, and because all the stores were made of wood and covered with vinyl, the fire swept throughout the market quickly. Along with the entire market, my little store also burned down in minutes. I became penniless overnight again.

Everyone contributed their resources to restore the market. There were many issues with ownership rights. Therefore, we had to establish our rights along with the other vendors in the market.

I was able to get the necessary items to restart the street vendor shop. The market was newly organized after the fire, and it attracted many shoppers. People around us then said this was all due to the good woman that had come into my house, bringing good fortune to all around her.

Our story took centre stage of the neighbourhood gossip in a positive way, and it also brought many people to our church, Suwon First Church.

Things began to look up for us. Little by little, we saved enough money and entered into a contract with the owner of the street vendor. It was a small store, but it was ours now. We were proud to own it. I came to the south with nothing in my pocket, and now, along with my good wife, we purchased this store. The store had five outer doors that were made of galvanized steel, and each door had a number assigned to it, 1 to 5. When the last door was closed, I could lock all the doors to the store with one key. The day I became the owner of this small store was the day a famous businessman, Chairman Byung Chul Lee, became the owner of one of the biggest conglomerates in Seoul, Korea. It made the headlines in the newspapers.

I did not envy that famous businessman, Chairman Lee. What I had was a miracle and God's blessing. I can't tell you how happy I was. I would go out in the middle of the night to look at the store we had just purchased. This was an answer to my wife's prayers, so it felt so much more special as if we had been given both heaven and earth.

Our store now was firmly established in the middle of the Yeongdong Market in Suwon city. The name of the store was Sangsin Trading Company.

People called me Owner Lee after having called me Deacon Lee from Hwanghae Province. My wife was now called Madam Lee, with much admiration by the people around us in the market.

I realized that God held my hand even in the darkest times of my life and did not let my hand go, not even for a second. He was always with me. My heart raced, thinking about opening the five doors to the store the next day, and the day after that, and the day after that. We were very happy. The church members were also very happy.

In the fifties, after the war, many tent churches were raised without obtaining any permits. If a minister saw a good piece of land, he and his church members put up the tent, and it became a church. The authorities frequently threatened to tear them down, but there weren't enough public workers to enforce what they threatened to do.

Suwon First Church bought a little piece of land to build a church, and we also bought some adjoining government land that was about two thousand square feet.

There were no schools to provide education, and many social organizations opened their doors to educate those that were poor and had nowhere else to go to receive an education. The services they provided were like lamplights shining in the dark.

We built our own church and built a two-room school to provide evening classes for those in need, and my first son became its first student.

I have three children from the north, and three children from the south, six children altogether. Each child is like a finger on my hands. If I bite any finger, it would hurt, no matter which finger.

I love all my children, and I would like to spend a little time talking about my oldest son, who now lives in Chicago. He is over eighty years old and is an elder in his church. His name is Hyosub Lee. In many families, it was frequently the first child that became the sacrificial lamb if the parents were not able to care for the younger siblings. And this was the case for Hyosub.

He had no choice but to come to the south with his mother and two younger siblings, crossing the 38th parallel and risking his life. Then when he was just getting settled, his mother suddenly died. He then had a stepmother and had three more siblings within five years. Because of the difficult circumstances we were in, he had to look after his five younger siblings. He did not go through the typical teenage years.

When Hyosub was about fifteen years old, we were in the middle of building Suwon First Church. The US Army in Osan City donated building supplies, and the supplies and materials were all spread out in the middle of the construction site. Anybody could walk in and take the building materials, especially at night. So, we had Hyosub as the watchman during the night. In the winter, when it was freezing cold, he'd sit by a small bonfire, staying up all night. In the morning, one of the elders would come and give him a little chunk of pork in appreciation for his work. Hyosub would go home with the meat, and by that time, I was already at the store with my wife, running the small business. Hyosub would cut the meat and grill it, then have his siblings line up, and he would feed them one by one, without feeding himself any. He was like a mother bird feeding the baby birds, and the baby birds didn't take their eyes off their mother bird. He was at an age where he must have been starving for some meat, but he saved all the meat for his younger siblings. My heart aches and goes numb every time I think about the sacrifices he made.

There is an old saying that one's first child is sent from heaven. Hyosub did not get the heavenly treatment, however. He was not able to receive the kind of education that his five younger siblings did.

All of the younger siblings were able to attend universities or colleges and beyond, but Hyosub only received two years of schooling from Jydong Elementary School, and he also took some evening classes. That is all the formal education he was able to receive. He devoted his teenage years to taking care of the younger siblings and helping my wife and me with the market business and the church building.

When the second church was being built in Suwon, Hyosub rode a motorcycle up and down a crooked hill to travel to Seoul from Gunpo city to pick up church building materials. He didn't complain about the number of trips he had to make, and he didn't complain about what time of the day or night the trips had to be made. He had opportunities to goof off with his friends, who just hung around, doing nothing. And he could have easily gone sideways but he did not, and he kept his faith in God.

As time passed, my mother-in-law in Pyeongtaek recognized and appreciated Hyosub's devotion to his stepmother and to his younger siblings. For Hyosub's birthday every year until Hyosub was married, my mother-in-law brought a chicken to my house, cooked it for Hyosub and set his birthday dinner table.

Through this story, I want to say that I appreciate all my children. However, it was Hyosub's quiet obedience in fulfilling his duty as the first son that allowed me and my wife to run the business and attend to the church business. I feel I have given him nothing, but God gave him many blessings.

Hyosub was led to come to the United States some twenty-six-plus years ago. Hyosub's first son resides with his parents and works at a local market, packaging products. His second son is a pharmacist, and the third son is a lawyer in private practice. They all live in Chicago. It comforts me to know Hyosub lived through difficult times but came through it with much success.

JOURNAL ENTRY PUBLISHED DECEMBER 9, 2017:
OUR OWN HOUSE

My family grew in size, but we had no house to call our own. My wife and I prayed, "Lord, you gave us our own store. Can you give us a house where we can shelter away from the wind and rain?"

When the North refugees poured into the south, the South Koreans gave an incredible amount of support to the refugees. However, there were many southerners who carried negative views of the refugees for being too ferocious in their daily struggle to live and feed their children. It is part of human nature to be in conflict when one's survival is concerned. These negative views and conflicts filtered into the churches and surfaced within the church.

This kind of conflict was part of the reason for building Suwon First Church. We formally registered our existing church with the city. Many refugees were already Christians due to the earlier introduction of Christianity to the north, then to the south. We could have grown stronger together in our faith.

Instead, the southerners in the church snubbed the refugees and distanced themselves from us. Even the designated duties with titles for the refugees as elders or deacons were ignored and dismissed by the southerners. I am not here to criticize anybody, but there were many refugees who went to church and received more pain from snobbery and dismissiveness than peace.

This may be why one of the biggest churches in Korea, Yeong Nak Church, started with refugees as its primary members. Yeong Nak Church gathered the refugees in every big city in the south and spread the Gospel. This also caused Christianity to grow and expand in the south in ways that were not anticipated.

We had our private land, and we purchased additional land for Suwon First Church. The land was big enough to build a church, an adjoining parish for the pastor, and there still remained enough land for some housing.

All the elders and deacons in the church were refugees from the north, having left their homes with nothing in their pockets. So, we had a meeting and came to an agreement to divide the remaining land and build seven houses.

The only problem with building a house was that it had to be built in one day, and the family had to move in at the end of that day. The land was not under our names, and we had no permits to build homes. So, within a day, we put together a shack with scraps of wood to avoid the wind and covered the roof with flattened boxes. And we all moved in at the end of the day to avoid the demolition of the site.

The district officers came out to the site to approve the demolition of the shacks built in one day, but when they saw the children lying in each shack side by side, they turned their eyes and went back to their offices. They pretended not to know the existence of the illegally built shacks and tacitly approved the site.

Once the officers left us alone, we replaced the rooftops with metal sheets. The metal roof created quite a noise when it rained. The raindrops were loud and sounded thunderous. When the winds blew harshly, rooftops flew away. But we survived through it all and secured a home for our family.

The house with a flattened box for a roof was memorable. A few years ago, I saw in the news on TV the refugee camps built in Ethiopia. The camps were built with flattened box rooftops, resembling the box roof houses we had built in one day. Watching the news brought back fond memories.

JOURNAL ENTRY PUBLISHED DECEMBER 16, 2021: MR. PARK SHARES HIS IDEAS FOR A NEW BUSINESS

Now that we owned our little house and our little store, we were finding some stability in our lives, away from the years of destitution and distress. To accomplish my intended mission, my wife and I started a period of twenty-one days of prayer, as Daniel did in the Bible. This was a prayer of petition and supplication, and we were determined to receive an answer from God.

On the last day of our prayer period, we received assurance from God that He would send a very precious person to help us accomplish our mission.

We waited all day, our hearts restless and fluttering with much anticipation. We were waiting for some great man when Mr. Park from Pyongan Province suddenly walked into our store. He was a deacon at a church, someone we didn't know well, but we were acquainted with him. The minute he walked in, I knew in my heart that he was the person God had sent in response to our prayers.

Mr. Park did not have a good reputation among the people in our market streets. Many people called him a con man, a swindler, unreliable, and he evidently had no credibility. Without prompting, he blurted out that he wanted to go into a business with me, making long underclothes like the long johns that one wears in the winter.

Really? Was this the answer from God? During my lifetime, I had not engaged in ignoring people or being prejudicial toward those that had less social or financial status. But I did not understand why, of all people, God sent someone that was penniless and had a swindler's reputation when there were plenty of people with some money and better reputations.

My wife and I didn't understand why we were engaged in a business in which we had no experience, which we also felt had less than a ten percent chance of succeeding. We both felt like we had been swept up into the situation, like floating down the uncontrollable river currents. We both stared blankly at our situation and felt as if we were standing before the parting of the Red Sea, trying to make some sense of the situation.

Mr. Park's condition for doing the business with me was that he would provide the technology and the know-how of the business, and I would provide the financial support. I said I had no experience or knowledge of running that kind of business. He said we should go to Yeongdeungpo junkyard and take the machines that had been thrown away and buy the scraps and things to fix the machines. He said two machines would be more than enough to run the business he had in mind. Within two hours of talking, Mr. Park took me to the junkyard, and we bought two big machines, covered with red rust from rain and the passage of time. I paid one percent of the price of new machines.

Mr. Park was obviously very good at talking. He used that talent and somehow found an empty lot belonging to the city, near the Suwon train station. The lot size was about thirteen hundred square feet. Before anyone could object, he put up a tent on the lot, and there he stored the two machines.

The two broken machines took almost all the space in the lot under the tent Mr. Park had built overnight. Now it was time to dismantle the rusted machines, clean them, oil them, and restore them to working condition. Mr. Park spent several days and nights fixing the machines. I didn't know a thing about how to help him, so I walked around the machines, praying all the time, "Lord, with these machines, let me build ten churches!" Mr. Park would get upset with me for doing this while he was trying to repair the machines and routinely cussed at me in his North Korean accent, "Get out of my sight, you little bitch!"

The machine's name was "Daimaru." It was terminology I had never heard before, as I was in the apple orchard business. The machine was huge. It had about twenty thread yarn bundles hanging from it, and once the machine was turned on, the yarn bundles would spin, and the threads spun down to weave a fabric that then came down to the bottom part of the machine.

We purchased the threads from a thread factory, along with the necessary items to make the underclothing, but we could not find anyone knowledgeable in Suwon who could operate these machines. So, we brought in ten workers from Seoul, with conditions that were acceptable to them.

JOURNAL ENTRY PUBLISHED DECEMBER 23, 2017: BLOSSOMING OF THE NEW BUSINESS

For the first time since being in the south, I used my credit to borrow money from here and there to establish a working factory. In front of all the employees, we turned on the first machine. It made noises. Threads flowed down from the thread bundles hanging from the machine. And when I saw bright, shining white fabric coming out, all woven by the machine, my eyes suddenly welled up with tears. It felt as if money was pouring out of the machine. Hallelujah!

Even though I did not own the lot where the factory stood, Mr. Park and I hung a sign that said "Sangsin Textile Company."

I received congratulatory greetings from surrounding people for becoming an owner of a factory. They saw this as an elevated position from being a shop owner in the market, but to me it was just a title, and I still could not tell if what I was doing was part of God's answer to our prayers. The reason I doubted God's answer was due to my lack of experience and knowledge in running this kind of business. I was completely ignorant. For example, Mr. Park would tell me to go right away to Yeoungdeongpo and bring him one "neonbari," and two "ohbaroke," but what were they for and what did they look like? I had no clue.

Mr. Park, who people believed to be a swindler, was he the answer to my twenty-one days of prayer?

It took me several months to realize that God sent Mr. Park. The minute I realized this great blessing, I was so overwhelmed with fear of God, I just broke down and cried.

I had cried many times throughout the war. I cried when I had to leave the north without my family and cried endlessly when times were hard. But these were tears of reverence toward God.

It dawned on me that God took Mr. Park's hand, a man with no status or position in society, a man that people avoided, and brought him to me. This reminded me of Jesus taking the sick and weak ones to his bosom in Galilee and healing them, like Mr. Park taking the old and broken machines and fixing them. Once I realized God's providence in his blessing me with Mr. Park, I spent many nights crying in gratitude.

If you're poor and don't keep small promises, people immediately judge you as a swindler. If you're rich and forget to keep the promises, people say you must have forgotten. Those were hard times when refugees were judged poorly and with severity. Mr. Park was not a swindler. He was a refugee who had five children to feed and raise. He was hustling and doing what he could to avoid starvation for himself and his children.

From that point on, I began to live respecting the weak and avoiding the strong.

I made so much money from this new business. Using the exchange rate of the time, I made somewhere around seventy million dollars. I served as the president of the Kyunggi Province Textile Association for three years.

All the powerful political figures, such as congressmen, mayors, and governors, wanted to meet me, but I avoided the meetings. I also received many invitations from people with high positions in the Christian community. They were all lined up to meet me, inviting me to expensive hotels for meals, but I declined all the invitations.

Instead, I practiced the lesson I learned from Jesus through Mr. Park.

My neighbours were those in the Yeongdong Market, my fellow church members, and all the employees that worked for me. The ministers that I helped were those that were serving God in remote islands or in poor farming villages. I did not meet those that were established and secure. But I went to the poor villages and islands, sometimes changing boats several times, to assist the poor ministers in those areas.

We fixed leaky church roofs, built restrooms, and bought pulpits for the churches. We built the bell towers and bought the church bells. We bought organs for the churches. We also fixed the parish the ministers were living in and encouraged them to keep it ongoing. I only wish our children would live a humble life like that.

Somebody asked me a question some time ago. Outside of the family, to whom am I forever grateful? I said there are two people. The first person is the underground guide, who brought my first wife and the three children from the north to the south during the war, crossing the 38th parallel. I don't even know his face. The second person I am forever grateful to is Mr. Park, the factory manager, who walked back and forth within the factory like a tiger, yelling instructions to the workers like an army sergeant.

I want to return to talk about the new business I started. The factory was large by today's standard, but I did not have to invest very much. This was because the new liberal ruling party was ending its term, and the government was in a confused state. I didn't spend any money on the land. The land belonged to the government. All the machines I purchased were used machines that cost ten percent of the new machines.

But pulling together the funds to invest in the business was difficult because I had so little money of my own.

Within twenty days of opening the factory, the first merchandise, the long underwear, was produced. It was red in colour, and at that time, it was considered a filial duty to give a set of red two-piece long underwear to one's parents as a gift. The final process was to put the rubber band around the waist. When this was completed, one of the employees handed me the first set, saying this was our first product.

I put our first product up to my face and felt the softness and warmth of the fabric. Because it was new, it smelled fresh.

Within seconds, I thought of my parents, who had sold their apple orchard, their entire livelihood, to send their daughter-in-law to find me. It made me weep, thinking about my parents never having worn this kind of warm and soft long underwear. They always wore long underwear that was pieced together with various cotton materials.

I wanted to run to my parents with the long underwear that had just been manufactured in my factory. At that moment, I wanted to tell them that I had come to the south as a refugee with nothing in my pocket and brag about my latest success. I desperately wished that I could have presented them with a set of long underwear.

Tears flowed down my cheeks like rain. The employees did not know why I was weeping and asked, "Is it that nice?" I did not explain but brought our first product to my office and wept. If I could just once give my father this long underwear, I would have desired nothing else.

JOURNAL ENTRY PUBLISHED DECEMBER 30, 2017: MANAGING THE EMPLOYEES

As a Christian, I felt in my bones the difficulty in managing and administering the business. It was hardest to manage the employees. This was true especially when I lived by faith, attempting to surround people with love.

We did not have many holidays. Everybody worked day and night those days to avoid further destitution. It was normal to work seven days a week, and it was also normal for schools to be open on Saturdays. My wife and I made an announcement to our employees that Sunday was the Sabbath, a rest day, and everybody was to take the day off. It was important to run a good business, but it was more important for us to keep the Sabbath.

We prayed for each of our employees by their name every day that they may know God. Most of the employees started to attend the Suwon Second Church on Sundays, and many registered as church members. As a result, the church grew rather quickly.

There is an old saying that the wind cannot sleep when there are many branches. Managing one hundred employees was not an easy task. Those employees living out of town were given room and board. Those lacking an education were given the opportunity to attend night classes.

The pain of poverty began to ease and heal. Many employees were growing in faith. The business we had started in the south became a place that shared and spread the gospel. My wife and I were exhausted most of the time, but our gratefulness to God for the spiritual growth of our employees overflowed each day.

Everybody knew I gave them Sundays off to give them a chance to attend church. Many believers in the company attended our church, and even those that didn't want to attend the church came anyway, out of respect for me. Many listened to hymns while they worked, and the workers began to look out for each other, caring for one another.

I tried to care for the employees as if they were part of my family. But one day, something unexpected unfolded right before my eyes. The second factory supervisor came to me and reported that there were two thieves among the sewing group. He said the two thieves conspired each day to steal one set of the product, which was the same as half of their monthly earnings. The memory of what happened at the time is etched in my mind.

I was very upset upon hearing this news. I yelled at the second supervisor to resign his post, pushing a blank piece of paper toward him for his resignation letter. I said, "Thievery is bad, but you're the supervisor. Telling on them is worse than the thievery that is being committed." I then said, "I don't need supervisors like you."

The supervisor got down on his knees and apologized for reporting such unacceptable conduct. He knew there was no other place like my company that paid well and always on time and gave Sundays off. We made a promise not to allow incidents like this to happen again.

My wife was listening to all this. The two girls who were stealing had sick parents they were taking care of and also had four younger siblings living at home. The desperate situation and poverty had driven them to steal. My wife and I agreed we should pretend not to know.

From that point on, my wife would buy warm bread, sprinkle sugar onto it, wrap the bread in a wrapper, and slip the bread into their pockets when no one was looking. The following day, she would bake yams and slip them into their pockets when no one was looking.

I didn't ask my wife to do any of these things, but it warmed my heart to watch her approach the poor working girls this way. It was like watching a gracious evangelist approach those in need, which is another reason my wife and I did not have big fights or arguments during our marriage. My wife was gracious.

This type of indirect approach worked well. We thought the girls hadn't committed the sin for themselves but for their families. However, they shouldn't have made the mistake of stealing the products. But given the situation, how could we not look after them?

A few years after this incident, the two girls who were called "thieves" came to our rescue in a big way. Our business had failed, and we had nothing left in our pockets. We had to start a new venture. The two girls played a significant role in our making a comeback. One of the girls later became one of the leaders in the church. She used her own money to feed several hundred people who were homeless and hungry. The other became president of the Ladies' Auxiliary in a church and volunteered many hours helping others. Both were blessed with children and prosperity.

Had we driven the poor girls into a corner as thieves and fired them at the time, I doubt they would have served God as they had later in their lives. They were like precious diamonds in the service of God.

How could we meet God face-to-face, and what good would come of building as many churches as we wanted, had we not made the choice that we made at that time? Thinking back on it, that was a pivotal moment.

I thought providing the employees with a good working environment with love,

care, and support would ensure the success of the business. However, I felt dark shadows looming over our direction.

Our merchandise had become well-known everywhere as the best product in the country. Two boxed sets of our product equalled the price of a big sack of rice, but we continued to receive many orders at this price. We had enough work with backorders waiting to be filled all the time.

But my tendency to sympathize with the refugees and my tender personality created problems for the company and me. Many refugees knew that I was a Christian and lived by faith. They started to come from everywhere and begged me to sell them the merchandise on credit. Many of them used our church members as part of their credit and for personal introductions. I felt I was forced into a position where I could not refuse them. They brought their little children, telling me that they had starved for a few days, begging me for help, with tears in their eyes. I could not refuse their request. I sold the merchandise on credit. As time went on, what had started as my attempt to help the refugees became the start of my business's demise. Once the refugees left with the merchandise, there was no more contact. These days, we have telephones and other ways to communicate. But during those days, there was no way to contact them. The only thing to do was to wait for them to pay me on their own accord.

My oldest son made a big fuss over the credit system I had created. "Why do you give them credit?" he would ask. "The kids are starving, they say," I would reply. My son and I fought every day over this, and I continued to promise not to give the merchandise on credit.

However, if they described my hometown bridge or mentioned a name of a distant relative, I'd cave in and give them the merchandise on credit. This happened repeatedly, and I ended up giving over two thousand items on credit.

My family was having a difficult time, and I ran around the country, looking for the debtors to collect what they owed me. When I finally found the whereabouts of some of them, I'd find several little children having starved for three days in a row. More often than not, I'd end up buying them a sack of rice instead of getting paid for the merchandise they had taken on credit. Running the business became increasingly difficult.

I ended up selling my store in Yeongdong Market so that I could avoid financial ruin for my employees and my customers.

I should have demanded payment before giving away the merchandise on credit, even when the refugees were crying and clinging to me. But my personality would not allow me to deny their pleadings. My heart was filled with regret, and I felt terrible, especially for my oldest son and my wife.

JOURNAL ENTRY PUBLISHED JANUARY 6, 2018: THE TRAIN WRECK

I heard from someone that one of the debtors lived in Yongin city, so I took the morning train from Suwon and told my family that I would be back in the evening. "I will go and collect the money and come back tonight so that we can pay all the employees tomorrow without fail," I said. I left the house praying that I would be back in the evening with the money.

Once I got to Yongin, I spent all day looking for the debtor but failed to find him. I was going to take the night train home, but somebody appeared and said to me that the debtor should return by midnight. So, I spent all evening shivering in cold weather, waiting, praying, remembering Bible verses, and singing hymns. I finally met him, but I had missed the night train. It turns out he had nothing. He was all out of money. I held the disappointment in my heart and took the train the next morning back to Suwon.

When I arrived at the Suwon train station, my whole family was there, hugging me and crying. Last night's train from Yongin had derailed, and more than a hundred people died. Because the accident had happened during the night, they couldn't see the bodies. My family had been certain I was dead. When they saw me arrive on the morning train, they were overcome with tears of joy and surprise.

All of a sudden, my mind became clear. I felt as if I had been hit with a lightning rod. If my prayers of yesterday had been answered, I would have died on the night train. I saw a new meaning of the cross. I had thought by building churches, I was doing God's work. I stood in front of the cross, crying. My priorities were all out of order. People didn't just die in the war I just went through. God didn't tell me only to build churches.

He only asked, "Do you love me?" and tears ran down my cheeks. And then He said, "I love you," and tears flowed again.

This was the first time I felt and understood the cross, and I shed many tears over the revelation.

JOURNAL ENTRY PUBLISHED JANUARY 13, 2018: CLOSING THE FACTORY

The business produced good merchandise and had dedicated workers. In that way, it was a successful business for sure. But having starved and shivered in the cold while crossing the 38th parallel, I could not turn away those poor refugees. They were desperate to ask for help, and there were so many in need. I eventually ran out of money to keep the business going, and Sangsin Textile Company ended in bankruptcy.

People wanted me to keep the business going with private loans since this was a profitable business. However, I realized that building churches with profit was not the objective.

The point was for me to gain a better understanding of God. I wanted to be more sincere in placing my trust in God. I also did not want to request private loans.

Winding down the business, I had built in three years took no time at all. I paid all the employees for their work before closing the factory. Mr. Park and I needed to wrap up our end of the business. As the factory manager, he had been paid a salary for three years. He felt bad that he had been part of giving away about forty percent of the merchandise on credit, which contributed to the bankruptcy. So, the conversation between us was amicable.

Mr. Park wanted the most expensive machine in the factory, called "neonbari," as his retirement pay from the company. That machine would have sold for seven sacks of rice, so I did not hesitate in giving it to him.

That was the last time we spoke and our last encounter. As time went on, I tried to find him, but I never saw Mr. Park again.

After saying goodbye to all the employees with tears in our eyes, I walked around the empty factory by myself. All was quiet. The noisy machines, the chatter of young working girls and their laughter were all gone. The place felt desolate as I sat there reflecting on what had gone wrong.

I did not regret closing the factory. It would have been greedy and unreasonable for me to borrow private money to continue running the business. Everything I had earned in the south was gone. Neither my house nor the factory was mine since the land still belonged to the government. I was left with nothing. At the lowest point of my life, I threw myself at the mercy of God with prayer.

It was an advantage to having been a refugee since I understood other refugees and their plight. I also understood the capacity of believers who exercised their faith at times like this. As I was praying in the empty factory, I remembered the bullets flying by me. I did not resent the people who took the merchandise on credit. Instead, I was grateful to them. Because of the war, they had become poor and desperate refugees. I was sure they had the intent to sell the merchandise and pay off their debts, but their immediate survival prevented them from doing so. They had to buy food to avoid starvation. They had to buy medication for the sick in their family. I was sure they didn't spend money on anything that was not essential. I knew that much as a refugee, having gone through several near-death experiences.

Next to the factory, Suwon Second Church stood quite empty since the factory workers who had attended the church no longer lived nearby. During a membership meeting one Sunday, a discussion took place about building a church using our own land. "Where is the land to build a church?" someone asked. Somebody else said, "Deacon Lee has a piece of land."

Then I remembered that I had bought a small piece of land up on the undeveloped hill some time ago, thinking someday I'd build a house for my family. I had paid a very small price for that piece of land. It was akin to thirty sets of our merchandise and akin to the price of ten sacks of barley.

As soon as I realized I had a piece of land, I volunteered to donate the land for building a church, even though I was completely bankrupt except for that little piece of land. I went to the registrar's office the next day and transferred the land to the church, and we had a groundbreaking service.

My oldest son, who had spent day and night working at the factory for the last three years, was very upset with me. He couldn't believe that I had given away the small piece of land I had bought to build a church that initially had been purchased to build a family home.

My son expressed his disappointment toward me and voluntarily enlisted in the army. He left the family.

After closing the factory and donating my land, my heart could not rest in peace, thinking about my son. He had left for the army, embracing much pain in his heart. He had worked so hard day and night. These days, army life is much easier, with a shorter service length and breathing room. But army life in the 1960s was very different.

Those days, if somebody got a draft notice, the whole family wailed. Army life consisted of hardships that were difficult to endure. The government did not have enough food to feed the army, so they were always hungry. There were also many accidents in the military.

As a father, I was restless, knowing my son had enlisted voluntarily to be in this challenging situation.

However, my faith did not falter. I was steadfast. I believed that everything that happened in my life, along with the difficulties I was facing with my business, my children's pain, and anything else that unfolded in my life, was within God's providence. This belief allowed me to strengthen my faith in God further.

In the midst of all these thoughts, there was one thing I kept on believing. I believed that I had lost everything and I was ruined. I was still immature in my faith, which I did not know at the time.

After finishing the process of transferring my land to the church, I sat in the empty factory one day, praying as I did every day. But that day, I heard a thunderous voice. It rebuked me for my immature faith and said, "I gave you many things." I responded, "I am ruined now." But I heard God's voice saying I was wrong in thinking that way.

All of a sudden, Mr. Park's face surfaced clearly in front of me. He was not just somebody I had crossed paths with. God had sent him to me so that God could use me as his instrument. This was a fact that became clear. It dawned on me that I had learned all the skills running a textile company for the last three years from Mr. Park. To produce the merchandise that we manufactured, I had to know everything.

Among other things, I had to know all the places and people in the industry, where to buy the parts, what components were needed, how to run the machines, and how to fix them if they broke. I had become an expert in organizing about thirty different vendors and manufacturers, and I could have obtained a job managing a big company like mine.

It also dawned on me that I had learned from the bottom up, from knowing nothing to knowing everything about the textile business.

I could fix machines that wove the original materials. In fact, I could restore any machine in the factory. I could even tell if something was wrong with the machine just by the sound of the running machine. I was like a master of these machines.

Another big thing that dawned on me was that I had learned the technique of dyeing. It usually took years to perfect the technique, but I learned it in three years. My son in the army had also mastered all the skills I had and was equipped with the knowledge I had. That was an uncanny realization.

Then I thought about all the people that had come into my life during the last three years. They had all left me for other jobs now, but we had developed binding relationships, even with the "thieves," and these were relationships money could not buy. I felt as though these people were like those in Romans 16, who were willing to put their necks out for Paul with their unyielding devotion.

God had taken me, an apple orchard businessman from the north, and taught me and trained me in running a textile business from beginning to end for three years.

It was Mr. Park who had imparted all this knowledge to me and then disappeared. I was flabbergasted at the sudden insight.

When I first met Mr. Park, I did not know what I know now. I had thought I was ruined, but I was not. God had equipped me with the skills to do his work. God had sent his angel in the form of a factory manager and had Mr. Park teach me everything I needed to know.

This realization had me cry and wail in the empty factory, and I saw myself maturing a little more in my faith, which filled me all the more with gratitude.

I understood that the blessings that come with encountering people were greater than anything else in the world. From that point on, I treasured people all the more. This was because the angels that I had met were the nameless, the poor, and the shabby-looking neighbours.

I know the phrase "lay down your burdens" or "let go, let God" are easy to say, but in reality, I couldn't fully realize them in my life. I was supposed to raise my arms and surrender to God and recite the fact that it is no longer I who live, but Christ who lives within me. But I still had not surrendered to God and could not demonstrate that with my actions.

Now was the time to sit in my empty factory, with all the machines quiet. It was time for me to look at myself, reflecting on my faith. As I emptied my heart, I was surprised at the peace that was filling my heart. My situation did not change. But for some reason, God's presence was filling my heart like waves rolling in from the ocean, and I felt very comforted.

All I did was empty my heart and "lay it down." It was like when Gehazi, Elisha's servant in the Bible, opened his spiritual eyes and saw the heavenly armies with horses and chariots of fire all around Elisha.

I felt my spiritual eyes open. The joy that came to me was overwhelming, and I could hardly contain that joy.

JOURNAL ENTRY PUBLISHED JANUARY 20, 2018:
RUBBER BOOTS

In that joyful state, I visited a wholesale store owner that I had used to purchase threads. He welcomed me and said he had been thinking about me a lot lately. He then said he had a suggestion.

"There is a big rubber factory in Seoul that could use the kind of fabric you used to make. They're looking for that kind of fabric to put inside the rubber boots they're making. You might want to be a supplier of the fabric," he said. I did not understand what he was saying because I had never heard of rubber boots needing the kind of fabric I used to produce. As I was hesitating, not knowing what to say, he quickly wrote a letter of recommendation.

As he handed me the letter, he said, "Go to Seoul and find the manager in charge of the material in the company, and talk to him." This rubber factory, Joil Rubber Company, was probably the biggest factory in South Korea at that time, with seven to eight thousand employees.

I went to Seoul immediately, found the manager, and met with him. Without much negotiating, we drafted a contract on the spot and signed it. And because Suwon was his hometown, and I was from there, he drafted the contract more in my favour. He ordered a huge quantity of the fabric to be delivered to his company right away.

All this happened in one day, with one letter of recommendation from one previous business connection I happened to visit that day. The contract gave me more than enough work for six months. It would take all the machines running day and night, weaving the fabric, to complete the work.

The order was huge, but weaving the fabric to put inside the rubber boots didn't require as many employees as to when we were producing long underwear sets. This was a more straightforward and easier process.

The volume of the fabric we were to produce under the contract was equivalent to making several thousand sets of long underwear.

As this miracle unfolded before me, I remembered the Holy Spirit I had encountered that morning. Did I really fully surrender everything in my heart to God, or was I overwhelmed by the contract I had just received? I could not tell. I was so excited. I had to stop and look at myself. I then made a promise.

I said to myself that there was nothing I could do by myself. Everything is done by the Lord, whom I love. Everything. Making money, growing a business, and even building churches are all done by the Lord. I had to die completely, let God live within me, and let him do his thing. I vowed to follow this promise.

Ten former employees ran over to the factory within minutes of my obtaining the contract. They said they would report for work the next day. I was overcome with gratitude, and I was crying inside. I was ruined. My company was ruined. Yet they placed so much trust and confidence in me. All these relationships were formed by the former factory manager, Mr. Park. I thought of him again and his role in creating this type of relationship between the former employees and me.

Regardless of this new business outcome, I vowed to treat them as I would like to treat God, for the workers were sent from God.

Sangsin Textile Company opened its doors for the second time. The machines began operating, and the factory was filled with the operating noise, and all could be heard from outside.

JOURNAL ENTRY PUBLISHED JANUARY 27, 2018: HEAVEN'S DOOR OPENING

"Humble yourselves, therefore, under the mighty hand of God, that He may exalt you at the proper time." 1 Peter 5:6 CSB

I had lived a simple country boy life at the foot of Guwol Mountain in Hwanghae Province, digging for the wild vegetables, gathering firewood, and farming apples. Of course, I met many hardships after that period, but it was now time to reveal God's blessings, just like in the Bible.

I obtained another contract from a big company, Dong Shin Chemical Company. This company gave me the same favourable terms in the contract as Joil Rubber Company had. I had the original fabrics rolled, and each roll of fabric was measured exactly the same so that the final product in one box would have fifty rolls, totalling about eighty-eight pounds. The boxes were delivered to the two companies every other day. In exchange, the two companies gave me certified postdated checks as payments.

At that time, we did not have conglomerates such as Samsung or Hyundai, but these two companies carried similar weight as the big conglomerates do now, and all banks honoured their certified postdated checks. I could walk into any bank and exchange the checks for cash anytime I wanted.

Somebody said that you could work all your life trying to make money in a business, but the actual period for making money is about five years during the life of a business. You have to be at the right place at the right time.

These days, nobody would buy the kind of product I was making, but it was like going fishing in a big pond brimming with various fishes those days.

Most of the people in Korea at that time had to wear rubber boots. They were dressed in the white cotton traditional Korean wardrobe, but the roads were unpaved, and the mud was not covered with an asphalt like it is these days.

In the winter, people had to wear rubber boots to walk in the snow, and after the snow melted, they had to wear boots to go outside. After early summer, the roads were flooded from heavy rain, and the rain lasted for a long time. All the streets were covered with mud, and you had to wear rubber boots if you didn't want to have dirt on your clothes.

So, several hundred shoe factory owners from all over the country brought their bags of cash, wanting to purchase these rubber boots. They made unreasonable demands. They refused to buy any shoes unless they were allowed to purchase the boots first.

I was not a rubber boot maker. I only produced the fabric that went into the rubber boots. But my company was the only company in the country that made this fabric, monopolizing the whole industry. Making fabric for the boots was much easier than making long underwear sets. I didn't need as many employees. I only needed about a third of the employees for the boot fabric-making process.

Dyeing the fabric was easier because nobody wanted sophisticated colouring for the fabric that goes into the boots. I also did not need expensive threads as I did for the long underwear, so my cost basis was a lot lower than before, and my net profit from this business was twice the profit I received from the long underwear business.

This business was given to me. There was no other explanation for the ease and the hefty profit. This was by God's grace, and His blessings were pouring down from heaven as if heaven's door opened. I had no doubt about it. Among believers, we talk about God's blessings. But what was happening to me was not just God's blessings. The blessings that came down were over the top. God's blessings were being poured down like heavy rain from heaven. I thought the money bags from heaven had holes in them. So much money was pouring down.

Time went by with much success in this business. My first son from the army returned home and saw the miracle of God's blessings. He said, "Father, you love God so much. Even when you were completely ruined, you offered your only asset, the land, to build a church. The Lord blessed you mightily!" He experienced the grace of God and expressed it in his confession.

When I was pursuing money, I could not see the money. Now that I wasn't thinking about money but only thinking about following God, money followed.

It is expected that a small business owner like me, with only thirty employees, to show respect for the big bosses in the big companies if the small business owner wants to continue to receive work orders.

It was customary for somebody in my position to pay close attention to the purchasing manager and even remember the manager's wife's birthday. That was how the power play worked, with a certain amount of oppression and expectation from those in power.

But God became involved and intervened and kept me away from engaging in that kind of power play. In the contract, I had the lower hand. I was the supplier, and the company was the purchaser. But in reality, I had the upper hand.

This was because every morning, the president of each company would kick the purchasing managers below their knee caps, demanding that they bring in the fabric ordered from my company on time. The presidents told the managers to bring their resignation letters if they failed. So, every morning, the managers of the two companies, each with ten thousand employees, would come to me and beg me to fill their orders on time. "President Lee, please save my life," they would say to me every morning.

God gave me the power to have the managers hired or fired. If I delayed the delivery even for one day, they would be fired. And whether or not the biggest rubber company in Korea operated smoothly or not depended on my timely production and delivery.

When I realized this fact, I was overcome with God's ways of handling things. God had heard my father's tearful prayers for me long ago in North Korea as I was pushed to the brink of death many times. God presented the current situation before me, and I felt God's love flowing into my body and soul. And I felt as if I did not do anything for God. This was not the time to jump with joy, I said to myself. The financial blessings, being poured down, created fear within me. I said to myself, "Material blessings are not mine. This is the work of the Lord."

From that point on, I vowed to prioritize spending the money by helping the needy and building churches.

I procured five more weaving machines for the company, and the thirty employees divided the twenty-four hours in a day into three shifts. The company was running at full capacity. And every day, the employees produced mounds of woven fabric. God provided everything I needed to run the business as I prayed for my needs each day.

JOURNAL ENTRY PUBLISHED FEBRUARY 3, 2018: MY FIRST VISIT TO THE IN-LAWS

It had been ten years since I met and married my wife. She missed her estranged family but could not visit because she had been disowned. We had many hardships in the beginning, but the fact that she couldn't go and visit them made my heart ache. But even in this matter, God became involved and solved the problem using an amazing method.

One day my company driver, Mr. Kim, came to me. Mr. Kim used to be a driver for a general in the army. The general summoned him and said he needed to sell his car in a hurry. The car was too fancy and expensive to be purchased by most people. The general offered to sell the car at half price and asked Mr. Kim to find a purchaser.

So, Mr. Kim came to me with the car because he felt it was a gift from God for me to have this car at half price. The car was very well kept since it was maintained by the army. It was a bright, shiny black car, and I ended up buying the most expensive car, New Crown, at half price. We did not have Hyundai, Kia, and Daewoo at the time. We had Corona, New Corona, Seventeen, and New Seventeen. And then there were regular Crown and New Crown cars. The New Crown was longer in length. The car was the most luxurious in its design out of all the cars on the market.

As a side note, the governor of Gyeonggi Province was driven in a New Crown vehicle, like my car, and there were maybe two or three other New Crown cars in the district. It was made in Japan, and even though my car was three years old, it had fewer than seven thousand miles on it, probably because we did not have highways or freeways to drive on during those days. It was practically a brand-new car. I talk about this car because it is related to my first visit to the in-laws.

I made interesting observations while riding in this car. There were checkpoints those days where the traffic cops or police would stop various cars to identify the drivers and the passengers. However, my car was never stopped. Instead, we were saluted when we were driving by. The license plate number on the governor of Gyeonggi Province's New Crown was 1000. My car's license plate number was 1002.

My car had tinted windows, so you couldn't see the inside passenger from outside. They must have thought I was a really important person with a high position and therefore did not stop me at the checkpoint, fearing that they might get into trouble for not recognizing the car and the passenger in it. That was the car culture at the time in South Korea.

I sent a message to the in-laws saying that we were coming to visit. On the day of the visit, Mr. Kim wore a brand-new suit and put on white gloves. He knew our circumstances and was overly excited to drive us to my wife's family. I sat next to him. My wife and my two daughters sat in the back seat. The three boys rode the company truck that was filled with presents for the in-laws.

In the truck, we loaded boxes of clothes for each member of the family and additional gifts such as ten cashmere blankets, two hind legs of a cow, half a pig, several boxes of a variety of fruits, and everything else that looked good in the market. I had bought presents that were worth one hundred times more than one employee's monthly salary. It was like Jacob returning home to his family in the book of Genesis.

I had always felt bad for my in-laws. They lost their precious first daughter to me, a poor refugee widower with three young children, who had nothing to offer except for a small street market vendor. I understood how they must have felt at the ill fate of their daughter and how they must have spent years in tears.

As we arrived in Pyeongtaek, the streets were filled with people greeting us. People said Pyeongtaek had never seen a car as nice as mine. My father-in-law and mother-in-law ran out of their house without their shoes on and immediately hugged all the children. The first thing they said was, "The Christ you believe in must be real!"

They said they had no idea a poor widower like me would become this rich. They thought their daughter would come to her senses after living with me for a little while, split up with me, and return home.

This was our first visit to my wife's family since our marriage thirteen years earlier. Our children were happy because they now had their mother's side of the family and the extended family as relatives. I appreciated my in-laws treating all the six children the same, without showing any prejudice against the first three from the north.

I still miss my in-laws, who later became Christians and exercised their faith every day. It was as if I was watching my parents up north live each day with their faith intact. It warmed my heart and brought me much happiness watching them come to Christ.

Following my wife's example, her family and relatives later accepted Christ as well, uprooting their deeply buried Confucian belief system. They all accepted Christ. The same God that I met and knew also met and accepted them. My in-laws planted the seeds of the gospel in Pyeongtaek. My father-in-law became active in the church and served as a deacon for ten years.

JOURNAL ENTRY PUBLISHED FEBRUARY 10, 2018:
BUILDING CHURCHES

Our church was a member of the Hapdong Assembly in Gyeonggi Province. If anyone needed help in building a church, everyone knew to look for me. That fact was widely spread. This could be why three to five pastors would come to me simultaneously. They would stay and pray with me in my tiny house. When the money was available, they took the money for building their churches, and another round of pastors would come to do the same thing. This rotation of pastors coming and going continued for ten years.

At the time, my daughter Sung Ja (Stephanie) was attending junior high school in Seoul and staying with a relative during the week. She would come home on weekends and had to greet all the new pastors. She couldn't let her hair down and relax and spend time with my wife and me. But she did not complain and showed fortitude in addressing the situation each weekend. We were always so proud of her.

We had pastors visit from farmlands and remote islands. We did not know their faces or names. But when we heard their testimonials, God led us to help them. We treated them like Elisha, God's servant, would have.

In the seventies, a New Village Movement was started by the government. Part of this movement consisted of paving the muddy roads and streets. But until then, when rubber boots became no longer necessary, I was extremely prosperous. Every week, money came in huge amounts, somewhere between $3,000 to $5,000. I could have bought a big piece of land in Yong In with that money, but I did not waiver.

The ministers who came to receive money often helped with the work in the factory, taking breaks from their prayer time. When it was time for them to leave, I gave them not only the money they needed for their church buildings, but also gave them their out-of-pocket costs, such as transportation expenses.

Nobody left empty-handed. But I told them not to leave their names or their contact information. I also told them not to remember me, and explained that this was my way of paying God back for all the blessings I had received.

Think about it. I had been a street vendor in Yeongdong Market. I starved most of the time and saved as much as I could, and all I could save was somewhere between thirty to fifty cents per day. But now, I was making a thousand dollars a day. Did I do that? Of course not.

I experienced the blessings expressed in many passages in the Bible. With those experiences, my faith could not be shaken. It wasn't because my faith was greater than that of anyone else, but the word of God was the living proof on which I relied, and it was where I placed my faith

As I look back, there are many things for which I thank God. One of them is that the pastors that came to me for help during those days were sincere in their faith.

These days I often hear about fraudulent pastors being involved in activities that are ungodly. Not only are they fraudulent toward the church, but also toward its members, and most of all, fraudulent toward God. I don't have any way of verifying all the facts presented in the news, but the current news is filled with stories of pastors. If one of those corrupt pastors had come to me for assistance during my time, I would have fainted on the spot. But all the pastors that came to me were from desolate places, who took the gospel to areas where no one wanted to go. Such earned my respect. I am convinced those pastors became the foundation of building the churches that have grown as successfully as they have today.

The pastors I encountered were not afraid of starvation. They were not afraid of persecution. In the name of the gospel, feces were thrown at them. In the name of the gospel, coal ashes were thrown at them. They were faithful pastors involved in destroying the shrines and replacing them with church bell towers.

It didn't matter to me that other people didn't help these pastors. I had to be involved and assist them. This was the promise I had made to God during the Korean War.

JOURNAL ENTRY PUBLISHED FEBRUARY 17, 2018:
MORE BLESSINGS FLOWING FROM HEAVEN

The financial blessings continued steadily. And I don't know why, but God must have been in a hurry because He started showering down financial blessings that just overflowed.

In 1966, we had a monsoon season that lasted for two months. Behind our factory, there was a steep cliff where we would hang the dyed fabric to dry in the sun. Once the fabrics were dry, we would weigh them and prepare them for delivery. But because of the monsoon that lasted for two months, the need for rubber boots doubled all over the country. The orders for the rubber boots doubled, and the orders for the fabric doubled. Everyone was in a state of emergency to fill the orders.

The purchasing managers from the two companies were all the more focused on securing the fabric they needed for the boots. They were so desperate, they took the wet fabrics, saying they would dry them themselves. At times, the two managers would push and pull to carry more fabric to their respective companies. They didn't care that the wet fabric weighed twice the weight of the dry fabric. They wanted to take the wet ones and pay the price of the wet fabric weight. There was no stopping them. From where I stood, our workforce was reduced by half, yet our invoices showed double the price of dry fabric. And as soon as the invoices were presented, they were all paid immediately by the accounting department.

Who in the world would accept that kind of deal under those terms and conditions? However, the purchasing managers from the two big companies in South Korea insisted on doing their business with me their way. We were to stand aside.

The purchasing managers then insisted on picking up the fabrics themselves. They didn't want us to deliver them to their companies anymore. So now they were doing all the transportation.

In three months, I made so much money, I could have purchased one-half of Gyeonggi Province. Tell me, who could have created this scenario? God took me from the apple orchard in Hwanghae Province, then brought Mr. Park to teach me the trade and planned the whole miracle. Hallelujah!

While all this was going on from the business end, we continued to have many visitors at our little home all the time from all over the country. They were poor ministers and female evangelists looking for financial support. Some ministers were very poor; they had walked a long way to my house even with no socks and shoes. Once they arrived, they expected to be served with food and then to return with some money. My wife was very busy preparing meals for them, cleaning up after them, and participating in their stories during the worship services. Our visitors were treated as if they were the owners of the house.

There were so many visitors at any given time. Some neighbours thought they were debt collectors. People in the Yeongdong Market continued to ask me why there were so many debt collectors in my house when my company was doing so well. It got to the point that I got irritated every time somebody stopped me to ask this question.

Most of the churches in Jeolla-do, Chungcheong-do, and Gangwon-do provinces were established in dilapidated houses or buildings that had been abandoned by farmers. The church members would repair them and add a sign with the church's name, and from that point on, that house or building would be a church. The churches had very few members and no pulpit, electric fans, and heating system.

The farmers were usually known for their kindness to strangers, but their belief system was rooted in Confucian and Buddhist teachings for generations. Every time a discussion of religion came up, their eyes would darken, and they would attack the Christians by throwing stones at them. These incidents happened frequently. From time to time, I would see a minister limping toward me after being beaten by the people in the neighbourhood. These ministers did not regret their choices.

Those days, the ministers did not receive any salary, bonuses or have health insurance or retirement plans, as we do now. But those ministers were dedicated to doing God's work and persevered with their faith in God but with empty pockets. It was as if I was watching Saint Paul coming to Lydia's house after being severely beaten in prison, as recorded in Philippians. It hurts me deeply even now, just thinking about it.

That is why I became involved in meeting the ministers with their requests and helped them with repairing or building the churches. And after I gave them the help they needed financially, I never met them again. This is so that the left-hand does not know what the right hand is doing, as the Lord taught us.

JOURNAL ENTRY PUBLISHED FEBRUARY 24, 2018: SUCCESS IS IN GOD'S HANDS

Human beings all run toward success. As I look back at my life, everything was in God's hands. I experienced this truth throughout my life, and I never want to forget that fact.

God gave me material wealth. When looking at today's technology, it is hard to understand how I was able to make that much money with the items we produced, using the method and the system of the time. During that period, God used me. That is why I was strict in keeping my original intent and not avoiding it. In fulfilling my original purpose, my life was not always filled with only good events, but it was a life filled with its ups and downs.

Because I was so determined to keep my promise to God and support churches that were poor and in need, I feel I did not show much consideration toward my family. I gave huge amounts of money to the ministers, whose faces I didn't know and never saw again, but I hardly gave them any money to my children. I was frugal with them to the point of counting pennies. Sometimes I wonder if the children felt bitter about it.

They did not complain at the time. But I thought about how they must have felt, and I always prayed, "Lord, please do not bring pain to their hearts due to the work I must do, but please bless them instead." I also had to finally surrender to God my family and their future.

I had very little time for my family due to a constant string of visitors who were in need of my help. However, I could not have focused on building and helping poor churches without my family's support and patience. I didn't do it alone, and my family sacrificed a great deal to accomplish the tasks I set out to do.

I have always been very proud of my children and their character, and when I go to heaven, I want to tell the Lord I lived on earth as a happy father with many blessings from my children.

I became well-known in my district because I was riding a nice car and had a high income. I became the president of a business association consisting of over one hundred related businesses in Gyeonggi Province.

My intent in getting involved as the president was to guide the association not only for the business profit but also to share a certain amount of personal beliefs with others. But the belief systems of believers and non-believers were very different, and the opinions we held were far and wide apart. For example, it is common sense that you need to turn the machines off to give them a rest so that they don't break down. It is also common sense to provide days off for the workers, to provide resting time so that they don't become exhausted, break down, and get sick.

At first, the association members all agreed that all of us would give our workers one day a week to rest, but many members did not keep that agreement. We then changed the agreement to provide the workers with rest every first and third Sunday and agreed to penalize those violating this agreement. But many did not abide by the agreement. Many businesses would close the doors of their factories or companies and continue to have the workers work on those two Sundays behind the closed doors. They had no Saturdays or any holidays to rest.

Now that I think about it, I don't understand why everybody had to work so hard all the time, but today's financial success in South Korea can probably be attributed to that work ethic. The government workers had Sundays off and worked a half-day on Saturdays. I understand that people are not working as hard these days and that it is becoming a problem.

In the midst of the work culture during that period, my company always closed on Sundays and let the workers rest. It was a Sabbath, and I believed in giving them a rest. As a result, my company was running very successfully.

Many banks wanted to form relationships with me for my business accounts, and many realtors approached me to buy land at low prices. The realtors said I needed to buy the land cheap now so that many years later when the land prices would skyrocket, I could build more churches. They also encouraged me to keep emergency funds for the business.

All this was absolutely true. And I was fully aware of what people said about buying land and keeping an emergency fund, having been a businessman for over ten years.

But one day, I closed my eyes and thought very hard about these suggestions and encouragements. If I had a hundred times more than I have now and became ridiculously rich, could I or would I be able to keep the promise I had made to God as I was crossing the 38th parallel with bullets flying by me?

I then remembered the Israelites crossing the wilderness. Perhaps somebody else could keep the promise with such an excessively rich status, but I did not have confidence that I would be able to keep my promise to God.

On top of all that, I was always frail and weak, and people around me said I would not live long. They said I probably wouldn't live long enough to celebrate my sixtieth birthday.

That was all the more reason why I rushed to support the ministers and churches in remote islands and rural areas. I wanted to keep my promise to God before I died and have no regrets when I stood before God.

JOURNAL ENTRY PUBLISHED MARCH 3, 2018: WINDING DOWN THE BUSINESS

By 1976, the New Village movement changed most of the muddy roads in the country to be paved and covered with asphalt. People no longer needed the rubber boots, and the orders from the rubber companies dropped to 10 percent of what they had been previously.

My company that once had been a booming business, naturally declined. I was also getting on in years, which weakened the business acumen I once possessed. My oldest son was independent with another kind of work. So, I handed the business over to my second son, who had just been discharged from the army.

I did not have any savings or any seed money to give him because I had not prepared for the financial future of the business. I had spent the earnings fulfilling my original promise to God. What my second son received from me was an empty bank account, an inventory that was 10 percent of what it had been in prior years, the factory building, and the old machines. After I had given away the business, I was empty-handed.

One poor minister from Jeju Island came to me after hearing about my work for the ministers through the grapevine. I had nothing to give him. I scraped together some money for his transportation expenses and had to send him away. I had helped several hundred ministers up to that time, but I could not help the last minister from Jeju Island.

From time to time, I think about that minister I couldn't help. I cannot forget it after all these years. Other people around me say that I gave away everything and lived by faith and that I did all that I could, so I should rest my mind from that one time I couldn't help. Sometimes I think, "I should have taken out a loan to help him."

After taking over the business, my second son worked very hard to sustain the business. However, he lacked the capital to further invest in new machines, and he could not compete with other companies that could acquire modernized technology and equipment. I felt bad that I could not help him more, but I realized that you cannot serve God and Mammon at the same time.

My son understood where I was coming from. All my children understood that I was fulfilling the promise I had made. They each formed their own personal relationship with God and did not wander from God and their faith. For me, this was the biggest blessing I had received in my life.

EPILOGUE

I hope what I said does not become misinterpreted as bragging. God used me the way He wanted to, and I sought to obey Him. That's a fact, and I appreciate the readers who will fully understand my intention in sharing my life story.

Several years ago, I was asked to give a personal testimony during the celebration of the one-hundredth anniversary of the Christian Business Association in South Korea. I declined the request because I thought my testimony would sound as if I were bragging.

I have shared many things in this story. There were things I did not want to talk about, especially the painful and embarrassing events that my children may have forgotten. However, I am sharing my story with the Koreans in Vancouver, Canada. I have confessed and disclosed all that is in my heart in this story.

Just like the Samaritan woman at the well, who had to truthfully disclose that she'd had many husbands, I have honestly confessed my life's journey. I have climbed many treacherous mountains and crossed many rivers that almost swallowed me.

Did you cry a lot when you first immigrated? Did you cry when the church you tried to build failed? This old man probably cried more than anybody. The Korean War made me cry. Parting with my family made me cry. Poverty made me cry. I cried a river in my lifetime.

But Jesus cried with me each time I cried, and he has cried with all of us and has been holding our hands. I wanted to share the love of Jesus through this writing.

I appreciate the readers allowing me to share my story from Amenida Seniors' Community in Vancouver, where I now reside with my wife.

Stay healthy and be victorious, and I wish you many blessings.

OPEN LETTER FROM DAUGHTER STEPHANIE

Most Beloved Father,

All of a sudden I am choking with tears as I sit at my desk to write this open letter.

I feel you are still near me, and if I ran over to Amenida Seniors' Community now, I would find you there with Mom, sitting across from each other, reading the Bible aloud. The thought that I may see you there makes me happy, but it makes me very emotional as I think of all the love you gave me and all the sacrifices you made on my behalf.

I appreciate the opportunity to take care of you at a later stage of my life after you and Mom moved to Canada to be near me. This opportunity brought me so many blessings. I can feel the blessings deep in my heart. It has been my privilege.

It turns out that I am writing this open letter during the season of Lent. I think about the creator of the universe, the Lord of our lives, who came to this world to save us from death. I reflect upon His life on this earth, going through all kinds of suffering and then ultimately going to the cross to die for us.

And I think about the abundant blessings you gave me throughout my life. The first and foremost blessing that God gave me was to come into the world as your daughter. You used to say you didn't do much for your six children and that you were sorry about that, but that is not true. You were warm, faithful, and sincere. You were our role model and the root of our growing faith in God.

I thought I knew all about you and your life, but as I read these articles that appeared in the newspaper, I realized how little I knew. I also tried to understand how you were feeling, as I remembered some of the events you described in your testimony. It made my heart ache, and at times it was so painful, I cried.

You were a faithful servant of God, carrying your faith like an innocent child. You abided by the Word of God and never negotiated with God. You were my father, who could not stand watching people in poverty and difficult situations. You had such empathy. As I read your testimony, memories of the events you described popped up in my mind one by one.

Father, do you remember when your primary doctor recommended heart surgery? You declined the surgery saying, "I am prepared to go to heaven!" We had no choice but to cancel the surgery then. And look at how healthy you have been for so many additional years!

You are a true witness to God's control of our lives. You were 106 years old, remembering your past as if it were yesterday.

I couldn't believe your power of recollection as I read the newspaper articles each week. Many people commented positively on the articles, telling me that your story moved them. Then I thought, God gave you this opportunity to further His work through you and to glorify Him.

I have so many things for which to thank you. But do you know what I thank you most for? I want to take this opportunity to tell you. As you know, I believe the most precious calling I have received is to be the conductor of the Vancouver Zion Mission Choir and also a church choir. The calling was to praise God and to give Him the glory.

I was only five years old when you brought me to a piano teacher. You had conducted a church choir ever since you were a young bachelor in your hometown in Hwanghae Province. Pianists were hard to find at that time, and you prayed that if you ever had a daughter, you vowed to teach her piano so that your daughter could become a church pianist and become God's instrument.

You did not forget your pledges of that time, even after going through the Korean War, leaving your entire family behind in your hometown. You went through much hardship, yet you remembered your prayers, and you gave me music training. For me, learning piano became a mandatory subject. I never doubted the instrument of my life to be used for God's glory. I cannot tell you what a great blessing this has been to me and to many others.

Many series of events, both big and small, came my way in life. I lacked faith and did not understand many things. But the most traumatic experience I went through was the death of Joseph, my first son. I lost all the light inside me, and I lost all hope. You saw me go through the trauma as I hit bottom. But I know it was yours and Mom's unceasing and entreating prayers that helped me climb out of the darkness.

Because of the music education you gave me, I was able to get up, hold onto God, and once again glorify God's name throughout the world with music. The Vancouver Zion Mission Choir receives invitations from around the world, and we praise God with our voices. I am used as God's instrument through music, as you had prayed.

Father! God took little me and is using me as a choir conductor. Thank you for your prayers and encouragements to become who I am today, walking the path of praising God through music.

When I go to Amenida to visit, I see you walking down the hallway. Your one hand tightly holding Mom's hand, and your other hand holding your cane. You are talking with each other. It is like seeing a picture God drew. It brings me much peace, and my heart floods with appreciation.

It must have been extremely difficult taking care of Mom as she has Alzheimer's disease. When your grandchildren worry and ask you, "Are you okay, Grandpa?" you always said, "Of course, I am okay," and your eyes shone with love for Mom. That was you, my father!

I am writing this open letter on behalf of all your six children living in Korea, Canada, and the USA. Until we meet again, please stay healthy and happy. We love you so much.

With much respect and love,

Your daughter, Sung Ja (Stephanie)

Sang Sun Lee and his wife, Seon Cha Lee in 2019

CPSIA information can be obtained
at www.ICGtesting.com
Printed in the USA
BVHW020604160422
634368BV00004B/14